D0401775

MEXICAN DELIGHTS
❖ ———————————————— ❖ ———————————————— ❖
A TREASURY OF FAVORITE MEXICAN RECIPES

BY DOROTHY K. HILBURN

Designed by Camelback Design Group, Inc., 8655 E. Via de Ventura, Suite G200, Scottsdale, Arizona 85258. Telephone: 602-948-4233. Distributed by Canyonlands Publications, 4860 N. Ken Morey Drive, Bellemont, Arizona 86015. Ordering information: (520) 779-3888.

Requests for additional information should be made to The Camelback/Canyonlands Venture at the address above, or call our toll free telephone number: 1-800-283-1983.

Library of Congress Catalog Number: 93-072733
ISBN Number: 1-879924-14-5

TABLE OF CONTENTS

BIENVENIDOS.

Welcome to *Mexican Delights*. It has been a privilege for me to have been able to study such a colorful and interesting culture through its food. Mexican people, and their food, have long been an influence in my life. As a child, I spent many hours in the kitchen of our Mexican neighbors watching flour tortillas being tossed and laid on the griddle to cook. I can still remember the taste of those fresh, hot buttered tortillas. Mexican cooking is as diverse as the many regions in Mexico and is a celebration of the people and the history of the country.

The Indians of historic Mexico lived on many of the same foods still prepared in Mexican kitchens today. Wild corn was first cultivated in Mexico thousands of years ago and is still a very important crop. Corn is used in recipes for everything from tortillas to beer. The creation of *masa*- which is corn dough used for making corn tortillas and tamales- is still one of the most important uses of corn today. Other foods available to the prehistoric Indians of Mexico were sweet potatoes, avocados, turkey, chiles, peanuts, beans, potatoes, squash, pumpkins cocoa, vanilla, melons, pineapples and tomatoes.

When Mexico was invaded by Spain in the 1500s, the Spanish Conquistadores were amazed by these new foods and took them back to Spain. The Spaniards' main contributions to the Indians' cuisine were domesticated animals. Pigs, sheep, cattle and goats brought the Indians meat and dairy products. Another very important addition was lard, from the pigs, which was incorporated into Indian cooking methods. The Spaniards also brought rice and wine to the Indians. When these two cultures became intertwined, a new culture, now known as Mexican, was created.

Mealtimes in Mexico are quite different than those followed in the United States. In many regions, Mexican people eat as many as five times a day, eating lightly at the beginning and end of the day with a large meal served in the early afternoon. The first meal of the day, *desayuno*, is simply a cup of coffee and a roll. Later in the morning they may have a larger meal, called *almuerzo*, of eggs, rice and beans. The main meal of the day is called *comida*, which is usually served around 2 or 3 o'clock in the afternoon. *Comida* often consists of several courses, starting with a soup, followed by a rice or pasta dish, an entrée, tortillas and beans. This large lunch is usually followed by the traditional afternoon siesta. In the early evening a cup of hot chocolate, or coffee, is served with a tamale or sweet roll. This light snack time is called *merienda*. And finally, at 9 or 10 o'clock in the evening, *cena*, or supper, is eaten and is generally leftovers from the main meal. On special days, such as a holiday or birthday, guests may be invited and a larger meal will be served, usually after 10 o'clock.

Mexico is made up of several regions. The northern most region is simply referred to as El Norte. This region encompasses the border states of Texas,

Previous pages: Taco and Tostada platter with garnishes.

New Mexico, Arizona and California on the U.S. side with the main cities in Northern Mexico being Monterrey, towards the east, Chihuahua, which is in the central area, and the Baja Peninsula which is on the west coast. Northern Mexico is known for beef, dates, and its large, thin flour tortillas. The cuisine here is similar to the Mexican food dishes prepared across the border.

The Pacific Coast region of Mexico is home to such cities as Mazatlán, Jalisco and Puerto Vallarta with Guadalajara a short distance inland. Many of Mexico's premier resorts lie in this region. The seafood is abundant and many of the country's fruits, grains and vegetables are grown here. Besides being an international playground, Guadalajara is famous for its culinary achievements. *Pozole*, a pork and hominy stew spiced with either *chile guajillo* or *chile de árbol* is a famous regional favorite served in several fine Guadalajaran restaurants.

The Bajio region is centered between the Northern Pacific Coast and the Southern Pacific Coast, running inland, and hosts Querétaro, Guanajuato and Morelia as its main states. Signs of the Old World Spanish influence still remain. Rice pudding, *arroz con leche*, is one of the dishes for which this area is renowned, as well as *pan de muerto*, bread for the dead, which on All Saints' Day is placed on the graves of deceased relatives.

The South and Pacific South Coast areas of Mexico, hosting Yucatán and Oaxaca respectively, are reputed to offer the most renowned dishes in Mexico. Yucatán, the land of the Mayas is known for its honey, the spice epazote, and its varied supplies of fish. Oaxaca is known for its *guacamole*, *negro moles* and its inclusion of insects in many dishes.

Central Mexico is the home of the cities Puebla and Veracruz. The Cholula pyramid and the Mayan murals of Cacaxtla can be found in Puebla. Puebla is famous for its mole poblano which is a combination of different spices, chiles, garlic, ground almonds, peanuts and chocolate blended into a thick sauce which is poured over meat or poultry. Veracruz is best known for its tropical fruits, coffee and red snapper.

When visiting any of these regions, make sure to try the local dishes. The people are friendly, the country beautiful, and the food is out of this world. In learning to prepare mexican dishes it is always helpful to have a basic understanding of the main ingredients used. The following paragraphs may help to identify common elements in Mexican cooking. Cilantro: Same as coriander. It is better when used while still fresh.

Chick Peas: Or garbanzo beans. Available in cans in most grocery stores.
Chorizo: A spicy Mexican sausage. Can be purchased in Mexican grocery stores and can be made with either pork or beef.
Chiles: There are a wide varieties of chiles grown both in the United States and throughout the regions of Mexico. Chile flavors run from mild

and sweet to hot, very hot, and even hotter. The sizes of chiles range from very small to very large. The general rule is that the larger the chile, the milder the flavor. Beware, however, as this is not always so. Every chile, even those picked from the same bush, has its own flavor and degree of heat. It is always helpful to test a small portion of your chile before committing it to your recipe. If you have a chile that is too hot, try soaking the peeled roasted chiles in salt water for at least 2 hours and then rinsing well it before using. You can also reduce the heat by using less of the amount called for in the recipe, or by substituting half of a sweet green pepper and half chile.

> **Jalapeño chiles** are small green chiles with a fiery flavor.
> **Chipotle chiles** are smoked and dried Jalapeno's that have a smoky flavor that is very hot.
> **California chiles**, also called Anaheim chiles, are large green chiles with a mild flavor.
> **Serrano chiles** are very small, green, thin and very hot.
> **Poblano chiles**, also called Anchos, are large and dark green with a mild flavor and are often used to make Chile Rellenos.
> Note: Not all chiles of the same type possess the same flavor. Sample all chiles before using.

Chili Powder: Ground dried Jalapeño peppers as well as other spices.
Jicama: A white root vegetable with brown skin.
Masa: Moist Mexican corn dough preparation used to make corn tortillas and tamales, can be found at most Mexican grocery stores.
Masa Flour: Instant corn flour for the preparation of corn tortillas.
Mole: Can be found commercially in powder or liquid form in Mexican groceries as Mole Poblano or Mole Verde.
Nopales: Pulpy prickly pear cactus leaves.
Tomatillos: A small tomato-like vegetable with an outer papery husk, if they are unavailable, use green tomatoes.

Acknowledgements

As with any project, there are those special people who help along the way. I'd like to thank my good friend, Mark Wylet, for his help during the photography sessions for the pictures in this book. They wouldn't be the same without him. Also, special thanks to Myrella, and Two Plates Full in Scottsdale, Arizona, whose beautiful platters, dishes and bowls were used throughout much of the photography.

A selection of ingredients used in Mexican cooking.

APERITIVOS Y BOTANAS
APPETIZERS AND SNACKS

Appetizers and snacks are an important part of any Mexican fiesta or gathering. A wide variety of festive foods are offered to tantalize the appetite and prepare guests for the feast to come. Many Mexican snack foods are simply smaller versions of main dishes, such as tamalitos (little tamales), taquitos (little tacos) and tostaditas (miniature tostadas). Often, foods served in Mexican restaurants in the United States as main courses, such as tacos are actually eaten as snacks or appetizers in Mexico. The following pages offer some tasty selections sure to please the most discerning Mexican food lovers.

❖————————————————❖————————————————❖

GUACAMOLE
AVOCADO DIP

A perennial favorite of both Norte-Americanos and Mexicans, Guacamole is a popular vegetable dip for parties and gatherings of any size.

INGREDIENTS:

2 ripe avocados
Juice from 1/2 lemon
1/2 onion, peeled and minced
1/4 teaspoon garlic powder

1/2 teaspoon chili powder
1/4 teaspoon salt
1 teaspoon Worcestershire sauce
1/2 tomato, diced

Scoop out flesh from the avocados and mash with a fork. Mix in lemon juice. Add onion, garlic and chili powders, salt, Worcestershire sauce and tomato and mix lightly. Chill and serve with corn chips. Makes 2 1/2 to 3 cups. Garnish serving dish with parsley, green onions or chiles.

❖————————————————❖————————————————❖

QUESADILLAS
CHEESE TURNOVERS

INGREDIENTS:

6 flour tortillas (any diameter)
4 ounces Cheddar or Longhorn cheese, shredded
1/2 teaspoon black pepper

4 ounces Monterey Jack cheese, shredded
1 4 ounce can green chiles, diced
1 cup salsa (See recipe page 19)

Preheat oven to 350°F. Spray a baking sheet with non-stick spray and cover with tortillas in a layer. Toss the cheeses together in a small bowl and sprinkle over tortillas. Season with pepper. Bake in oven until cheeses are melted. Sprinkle generously with green chiles and fold in half. Dip in your favorite salsa. Makes six Quesadillas.

Aperitivo de Chile y Tuna
Tuna and Chile Dip

An excellent example of the variety of foods in the Mexican diet. Using fresh ingredients is best, however, canned substitutions will do nicely.

INGREDIENTS:

1 7-ounce can tuna, drained
1 tablespoon olive oil
1/2 cup chopped onion
1/4 cup chopped jalapeno peppers
1/4 cup chopped scallions
1/2 cup capers, drained

1/3 cup chopped celery
1 chopped tomato
2 tablespoons lime or lemon juice
1/4 teaspoon seasoned salt
1/2 bag tortilla chips

Combine tuna, olive oil, onion, jalapeño peppers, scallions, capers, celery, tomato and lemon or lime juice. Salt with seasoned salt to taste. Toss to mix well. Garnish with grated cheese, serve with tortilla chips (Recipe on page 42.) Makes three cups.

❖ ——————————————————— ❖ ——————————————————— ❖

Buñuelos de Coliflor
Cauliflower Fritters

An unusual but tasty combination of pastry and vegetables. Fritters are usually a desert, but in this instance make a wonderful appetizer.

INGREDIENTS:

1 pound cauliflower, separated
1 egg
3/4 cup milk

3/4 cup flour
1 teaspoon sugar
3/4 teaspoon baking powder

Boil separated cauliflower in salted water for 6 to 7 minutes or until it's tender. Drain. Heat 1 inch oil in saucepan to 365°F. Beat egg and milk in a small bowl. Mix sugar, baking powder, flour, salt and nutmeg in a medium bowl. Stir milk mixture into flour mixture and beat until smooth. Dip cauliflower into batter. Fry in hot oil until light brown all over. Place on paper towels to drain excess oil. Serve while hot. Serves 6.

❖ ——————————————————— ❖ ——————————————————— ❖

Tostadas de Piñon
Roasted Piñon Nuts

Take one pound raw, shelled piñon nuts and spread evenly in a shallow baking pan. Roast in oven at 300° F for one hour. Stir frequently to brown nuts evenly. Serve as a snack.

Following Pages: A selection of Appetizers

TOSTADA DE QUESO
CHEESE CRISP

An open faced cheese and tortilla appetizer that has long been a favorite item at Mexican gatherings. Can be served as a snack or appetizer.

INGREDIENTS:

6 Flour Tortillas (bought or made from recipe on page 43)
1 1/2 cups Monterey Jack cheese, shredded

1 1/2 cups medium sharp Cheddar cheese, shredded
Guacamole (see page 10)
Salsa (see page 19)

Place tortillas on large baking sheet. Mix shredded cheeses in small bowl. Spread mixed cheeses evenly over tortillas. Place baking sheet in oven under broiler, or in microwave oven if mircowavable sheet is used, cook until cheese is melted. Garnish with avocado dip and/or salsa. Chile slices may be added. Cut in slices and serve.

❖————————————❖————————————❖

APERITIVO DE CHILE VERDE
GREEN CHILE DIP

A colorful and flavorful, but mild, chile and avocado dip that goes well with fresh vegetables as well as tortilla chips.

INGREDIENTS:

1 4-ounce can of green chiles, drained and chopped
1 avocado, diced

1 cup sour cream
1/2 teaspoon salt
1/2 teaspoon Tabasco sauce

Mix chiles, avocado, salt and Tabasco sauce in sour cream. Chill for 1 hour and serve with carrot or celery sticks or tortilla chips. Serves 8.

❖————————————❖————————————❖

APERITIVO DE CAMARONES
SHRIMP DIP

INGREDIENTS:

1/4 cup chili sauce
1 teaspoon horseradish
2 teaspoons lemon juice
1/4 teaspoon hot-pepper sauce

1 cup sour cream
1 4-ounce can shrimp, drained and chopped
Salt and pepper

Mix chili sauce, horseradish, lemon juice, dash of salt and pepper and hot-pepper sauce. Fold in sour cream and chopped shrimp. Chill for one hour and serve with corn chips or vegetables. Makes 1 3/4 cups.

NACHOS
TORTILLA CHIPS WITH MELTED CHEESE

The ultimate Mexican finger-food. Ideal for smaller gatherings.

INGREDIENTS:

6 corn tortillas (see page 42)
4 to 6 small serrano or jalapeño peppers, sliced

1 small tomato, finely chopped
1 small onion, finely chopped
3/4 cup cheddar cheese, shredded

Cut each tortilla into four pieces. Place pieces on a baking sheet and bake for five minutes in a 400°F oven until crisp. Pile tortilla chips together on a plate with all the chips touching. Spread the cheese, onion, tomatoes and peppers over the chips and place into an oven at 400°F. When the cheese is melted the Nachos are done - takes approximately 5 minutes.

❖————————————————❖————————————————❖

CAMARONES DIABLADOS
DEVILED SHRIMP

INGREDIENTS:

1/2 cup dry white wine
1/2 cup wine vinegar
2 tablespoons mustard
1 teaspoon horseradish
1/2 tablespoon paprika
1/2 teaspoon cayenne pepper

2 tablespoons catsup
1/4 teaspoon garlic powder
1 cup vegetable oil
1 pound cooked shrimp, cooked
1/2 teaspoon salt

In a large mixing bowl, combine white wine, vinegar, catsup, mustard, horseradish, garlic powder, cayenne pepper, paprika, oil and salt. Beat until blended well. Add shrimp to marinade and let sit for 3 hours in refrigerator. Drain shrimp and serve on a bed of lettuce.

❖————————————————❖————————————————❖

BUÑUELOS DE GARBANZO
CHICK PEA FRITTERS

INGREDIENTS:

2 cups chick-peas, cooked
1/4 cup onion, chopped fine
1/2 teaspoon pressed garlic
1/2 teaspoon baking powder

1/2 cup smoked ham, cut into small cubes
Olive oil for frying
Salt and pepper

Mash peas. Add onion, garlic, and baking powder and mix. Shape in small balls and press a cube of ham in center of ball. Roll mixture completely over ham. heat oil to 375°F and fry balls to a nice brown color.

CHILES Y SALSAS
CHILES AND SAUCES

C hiles are one of the most important and most often used ingredients in Mexican cooking. There are many different varieties of chiles, each with its own distinctive flavor. The flavors of chiles vary as much as their shapes and sizes. A common misconception about chiles is their heat. Not all chiles are fiery hot, many are very mild. The hottest part of the chile is the interior vein which houses a substance called capsaicin. The seeds and placenta are also very hot due to their close proximity to the capsaicin. Often the smallest chiles are the hottest. The most important thing to remember when handling chiles is to use rubber gloves and to make sure your hands do not come into contact with your eyes, mouth or nose. The eyes are especially sensitive to chile oils. Make sure to wash hands and gloves in soap and water after working with chiles.

❖―――――――――――❖―――――――――――❖

PREPARATION OF CHILES

Preparing fresh chiles is quite easy. Wash chile and dry well. Char the skin of the chile over a gas stove, barbecue, under a broiler, or in a heavy skillet. Turn often to blacken the skins evenly and prevent the flesh of the chile from burning. When the chile's skin is black and blistered place chile in a plastic or brown paper bag for 10 minutes. This allows the steam to loosen the skin from the chile. Charring the skins gives the chiles a very nice smokey flavor. Wearing rubber gloves, peel off loosened skin. If planning to use the chile whole, slit the side of the chile to remove seeds and stem. Rinse chile in cold water. Chiles can be frozen with or without the charred skin.

❖―――――――――――❖―――――――――――❖

SALSA DE CHIPOTLE
CHILE CHIPOTLE SAUCE

Chipotle chiles may be difficult to find, but they are certainly worth the trouble. They give this sauce a flavor unlike any other.

INGREDIENTS:

1 or more chile chipotle, chopped
1 can tomato sauce
1 can tomatoes, chopped

1 clove garlic, pressed
1 medium onion, chopped
2 tablespoons vegetable oil.
Salt and pepper

Saute onion in oil and add chile chipotle, tomato sauce, tomatoes, garlic and salt and pepper to taste. Cook for 20 minutes. Makes 1 quart.

A Selection of Fresh Chiles with Salsa de
Chipotle (Red) and Salsa Verde (Green).

SALSA DE TOMATILLO
TOMATILLO SAUCE

Tomatillos are an often used vegetable in Mexican cooking. Their bright green color and unique flavor make this sauce very popular.

INGREDIENTS:

6 tomatillos	1/4 teaspoon cumin
1/2 small onion, chopped	2 tablespoons water
4 serranos, chopped	2 tablespoons cilantro, chopped
1 garlic clove, chopped	Salt and pepper

Remove the outside skin and the stems from the tomatillos and rinse them in warm water. Simmer for 7 to 10 minutes. Put all ingredients in a food processor and process until the sauce reaches the desired consistency. Add water if necessary. Use extra cilantro leaves for decorative topping.

❖————————————❖————————————❖

SALSA VERDE
GREEN SAUCE

This tasty sauce is a standard at any Mexican table and is a perennial favorite of both Norte-Americanos and Mexicans.

1 can green chiles, peeled	2 tablespoons pumpkin seeds
3/4 cup parsley, chopped	1/4 cup oil
2 1/2 cups chicken broth	Salt and pepper

Toast pumpkin seeds in oven until lightly brown. Grind pumpkin seeds with chiles and parsley until fine using a grinder or blender. Grind two more times. Add 1/4 cup chicken broth and strain. Add strained mixture and leftover broth to hot oil and heat. Serve over chicken or fish. Makes almost 1 quart.

❖————————————❖————————————❖

SALSA A LA SUE
SUE'S SALSA

Our good friend, Sue Adams, claims this salsa is a scene stealer at all of her parties. We enjoy it, too.

1 16-ounce can chopped tomatoes	1/2 teaspoon cumin
2 4-ounce cans of green chile	1/2 teaspoon garlic powder
1 bunch green onions, chopped	Salt and pepper
2 beef boullion cubes	

Combine all ingredients and chill for one hour before serving.

Salsa de Pimienta y Tomate
Tomato and Pepper Sauce

Hot! Hot! Hot! This is one very spicy salsa that is guaranteed to light your fire. Make sure to have a Margarita handy.

INGREDIENTS:

6 jalapeno or serrano peppers, chopped
4 small tomatoes, chopped
1 small onion, chopped
1 garlic clove, chopped
1/4 teaspoon cumin

1/4 teaspoon black pepper
2 tablespoons of water (add more if needed)
Garlic powder to taste
Salt and pepper to taste

Chop peppers, tomatoes, onions and garlic and place in a food processor. Add spices and water. Process for 5 seconds before tasting. Add more water for a smoother consistency, if desired. Process for 10 seconds to finish. Add garlic powder and salt and pepper to taste.

❖————————————❖————————————❖

Salsa Roja
Red Pepper Sauce

A traditional red sauce from northern Mexico with a full flavor.

INGREDIENTS:

8 large red peppers
1 onion, chopped
1 clove garlic, chopped

1 cup water
1/2 teaspoon salt
Salt and pepper to taste

Simmer peppers, 1/2 onion and garlic clove in a saucepan for 20 minutes using enough water to cover contents. Drain the water, discard garlic and cool the peppers. When the peppers have cooled, remove the stems and slice peppers lengthwise. Remove seeds from the insides of the peppers. Put the peppers, remaining chopped onion and 1/2 cup of water into a blender. Blend until the contents become smooth. Add water if necessary.

❖————————————❖————————————❖

A WORD ABOUT CHILES:

Jalapeño chiles are small green chiles with a fiery flavor. Chipotle chiles are smoked and dried Jalapeno's that have a smoky flavor that is very hot. California chiles, also called Anaheim chiles, are large green chiles with a mild flavor. Serrano chiles are very small, green, thin and very hot. Poblano chiles, also called Anchos, are large and dark green with a very mild flavor and are often used to make Chile Rellenos. Not all chiles of the same type possess the same flavor. Sample before using.

PICO DE GALLO
ROOSTER'S BILL SALSA

Pico de Gallo usually includes jicama, which is difficult to find so we have omitted it. If jicama can be found in your area, go ahead and include it.

INGREDIENTS:

2 large tomatoes
4 jalapeno
1 medium onion
1/4 teaspoon garlic powder
1/2 tablespoon black pepper

1/4 cup cilantro
4 tablespoons water
1 tablespoon white wine vinegar
2 tablespoons lime juice
Salt

Cut tomatoes, onion, peppers and garlic into small pieces. Add salt and pepper and cilantro to the mix and continue to chop all ingredients together. Stir and let sit for one hour before serving. Put ingredients in a bowl and add the vinegar and water.

SALSA DE PEPINO Y MELON
CUCUMBER AND MELON SAUCE

A refreshing and unusual salsa with a colorful touch and fresh taste.

INGREDIENTS:

1 small cantaloupe
1 papaya
1 cucumber

1/3 cup mint
4 tablespoons lime juice
2 tablespoons honey

Dice cantaloupe, papaya, cucumber and mint, making sure to remove peeling and seeds. Mix lime juice and honey with fruit and chill before serving. Makes 4 cups.

SALSA PARA TACOS
SAUCE FOR TACOS

This versatile salsa can be used for dip as well as on Tacos and Tostadas.

INGREDIENTS:

2 cups canned tomatoes
1/2 medium onion, diced
1/4 teaspoon garlic powder
1/2 teaspoon oregano

2 canned green chiles, diced
1 dash hot sauce
1 teaspoon salt
1/2 teaspoon pepper

Add onion, chiles, garlic and tomatoes and mash until fine. Add oregano, hot sauce, salt and pepper. Mix well and chill before serving.

POLLO EN MOLE POBLANO
CHICKEN CHILE SAUCE

Mole Poblano makes a great sauce for Tostadas, served over hot rice or as a filling for Tamales. Turkey can be substituted for chicken.

INGREDIENTS:

5 ancho chiles, cleaned, seeded
1 large onion, chopped
1 16 ounce can cooked tomatoes
1 clove garlic,
1/2 cup salted peanuts
1 tortilla, cut in pieces
1/4 cup oil
2 tablespoons sesame seed
1/3 cup raisins
1 tablespoon sugar

1/4 teaspoon cloves
1/4 teaspoon anise
1/4 teaspoon cinnamon
1/4 teaspoon coriander
1/4 teaspoon cumin
1 cup chicken stock
1 square unsweetened chocolate
3 cups chicken, cubed
Salt
Pepper

Combine chiles, onion, tomatoes, garlic and peanuts, tortilla, sesame seed and raisins. In small amounts, blend to a thick purée. In a large skillet heat oil and add puree. Cook for 5 minutes, stirring constantly. Add sugar, cloves, anise, cinnamon, coriander, cumin and chicken stock. Bring to a boil and reduce heat. Simmer and add chocolate stirring until chocolate melts and blends with sauce. Add salt and pepper to taste. Stir in chicken pieces and simmer for 15 minutes. Makes 3 quarts.

SALSA DE CILANTRO
CILANTRO SAUCE

This salsa tastes great with shellfish and is also wonderful as a dip with tortilla chips. Try spooning this on top of nachos.

INGREDIENTS:

1 cup fresh cilantro, chopped
1 small onion, chopped
1/2 cup parsley, chopped
1/2 cup olive oil
5 tablespoons lime juice

3 tablespoons distilled white vinegar
1 jalapeno, cleaned and seeded
2 cloves garlic, minced
Salt

Combine cilantro, onion, parsley, oil, lime juice, vinegar, jalapeno, garlic and salt to taste. Mix well and refrigerate for 2 hours. Makes 2 cups.

A WORD ABOUT CHILES:

Poblano chiles, a dark green, heart shaped chile, when ripened and dried becomes an Ancho chile.

SOPAS Y ENSALADAS
SOUPS AND SALADS

Mexican soups and salads are as distinct as the rest of the Mexican menu. Recipes for special soups are handed down from generation to generation and prized by all. The unusual array or ingredients in many may seem a trifle odd at first glance, but are guaranteed to please even the most discerning palate. As the noted Norte Americano company, Campbell Soups has often said, "Soup is good food," and Mexican soups, although often overlooked in Mexican food restaurants, are certainly no exception to Campbell's golden rule.

❖————————————————❖————————————————❖

SOPA DE FRIJOL NEGRO
BLACK BEAN SOUP

This tasty bean soup is sweeping the Southwest and can be found in many of its finest restaurants.

INGREDIENTS:

1 pound dried black beans, washed thoroughly
2 quarts boiling water
2 tablespoons salt
1/8 teaspoon garlic powder
1 1/2 teaspoons cumin

1 1/2 teaspoons oregano
2 tablespoons white vinegar
10 tablespoons olive oil
1/2 lb. onion, peeled and chopped
1/2 pound green peppers, trimmed and chopped

Put beans in large pot and add boiling water. Boil for 2 minutes. Cover and remove from heat. Set aside for 1 hour. Add salt to beans and liquid. Bring to a boil and simmer, covered, for 2 hours, until beans are soft. Put the garlic, cumin, oregano and vinegar into blender and mix into a thick paste. Sauté onion and green pepper in olive oil until tender. Blend in the paste and stir mixture into the beans. Cook over low heat until ready to serve. Serves 6.

❖————————————————❖————————————————❖

SOPA DE AGUACATE
AVOCADO SOUP

INGREDIENTS:

2 ripe avocados, cut in slices
3 small onions, chopped
1/2 cup light cream

1/2 cup heavy cream
3/4 cup water
1 teaspoon each salt and pepper

Place avocados, onions and heavy cream in a blender. Blend until reaching a thick, smooth consistency. Add light cream, water, salt and pepper and puree until smooth. Add water to achieve a thinner consistency, if desired.

Sopa de Frijol Negro (Black Bean Soup) and Chile Cornbread

SOPA DE FRIJOL
BEAN SOUP

A Mexican staple that complements any Mexican fiesta.

INGREDIENTS:

2 cups canned kidney beans, undrained
1 cup beef stock
1 cup cooked tomatoes, undrained
1 clove garlic, minced

1/2 teaspoon oregano
1/2 teaspoon chili powder
Salt and pepper to taste
2 cups shredded lettuce
12 ripe olives

Place beans into a large saucepan. Mash with a fork or potato masher, leaving some large pieces. Add meat stock, tomatoes, garlic, oregano, and chili powder. Bring to a boil. Simmer on medium heat for 10 minutes, stir often. Add salt and pepper to taste. Serves 4.

SOPA DE QUESO Y CERVEZA
BEER AND CHEESE SOUP

A Mexican favorite with a little something extra. Quite popular while watching bull fights and soccer games.

1/2 cup chopped onion
2 tablespoons butter
1 12-ounce bottle of Mexican beer
1/2 cup celery, diced
1/2 cup carrots, diced

2 cups chicken broth
1 teaspoon salt
1 cup sour cream
1 1/2 cup Monterey Jack cheese
1/4 teaspoon nutmeg
1/2 teaspoon each salt and pepper

Sauté onion in butter until tender. Add beer and vegetables, stir gently. Bring to a boil and reduce heat before covering a let simmer for 7 to 10 minutes. Add chicken broth, nutmeg, salt and pepper. Bring to a boil and reduce heat. Simmer for 30 minutes, covered. Stir in sour cream when pot is removed from heat and garnish with cheese. Serves 6.

SOPA DE TORTILLA
TORTILLA SOUP

The perfect solution for what-to-do with those left over tortillas.

2 quarts chicken or beef stock
1/2 cup onion, chopped
1 cup canned tomato sauce
1 teaspoon salt
1/4 teaspoon pepper

6 or 8 stale tortillas
1 1/2 cups Monterey Jack cheese, shredded
Oil for frying

Heat stock with onion to boiling. Simmer on medium heat for 5 minutes. Stir in tomato sauce, salt and pepper and let simmer for 5 minutes. Cut tortillas into 1/2 inch strips and fry in hot oil until crisp. Place on paper towel to absorb excess oil. To serve soup, place a handful of tortilla strips in soup bowl and spoon soup into bowl. Sprinkle with cheese to garnish.

❖━━━━━━━━━━━━━━❖━━━━━━━━━━━━━━❖

GAZPACHO
COLD TOMATO SOUP

A tasty cold soup that's perfect for warm summer days.

INGREDIENTS:

10 ounces tomato juice
2 medium tomatoes, chopped
1 tablespoon sugar
1/4 teaspoon salt
1/4 cup red wine vinegar
1/4 cup salad oil

1 small onion, finely chopped
2 celery stalks, diced
2 green onions, chopped
1/2 medium cucumber, chopped
1 small green pepper, finely chopped

Blend together tomato juice, 1/2 of chopped tomatoes, sugar, salt, vinegar and oil in a blender. Add remaining tomatoes, onion, celery, cucumber and green pepper and mix well. Serve cold, add sour cream, croutons and shredded cheese to taste. Serves 6.

❖━━━━━━━━━━❖━━━━━━━━━━❖

CALDO DE QUESO
CHEESE SOUP

A thick, rich soup that makes a perfect main course, served with chili cornbread (see page 109) or tortillas, or a flavorful starter for any meal.

6 canned green chiles, peeled
1/2 pound Mexican White cheese
1 onion, minced
1/4 cup tomato sauce
1/4 cup milk

2 tablespoons oil
6 cups water
1 teaspoon salt
1/4 teaspoon pepper
5 medium potatoes

Peel and dice potatoes. Cook in oil until glazed. Add chiles, onion, tomato sauce, milk, water and cheese, crumbling cheese. Cook for 10 minutes, add salt and pepper to taste. Cook for 20 minutes. Serves 6.

❖━━━━━━━━━━━━━━❖━━━━━━━━━━━━━━❖

A WORD ABOUT ADDITIONAL SEASONING:

For additional flavor in Mexican soups add hot salsa or lime juice after serving to individual taste. Remember, a little hot salsa can go a long way.

SOPA DE LIMA
TORTILLA AND LIME SOUP

One of the best known Mexican soups, Sopa de Lima recipes originated in the Yucatán peninsula region of southern Mexico.

INGREDIENTS:

Oil for frying
1/2 cup onion, chopped
1/4 cup green chiles, chopped
2 corn tortillas
2 teaspoons vegetable oil
1 cup shredded chicken, cooked
(about 3 medium chicken breasts)

3 1/2 cups chicken broth
1 large tomato, chopped
1 tablespoon lime juice
1/2 lime sliced
Salt
Pepper

Cut tortillas in 1/2 inch wide strips and fry in hot oil until crisp, place on a stack of paper towels to absorb excess oil. In a large saucepan heat 2 tablespoons of oil and add onion and chile. Sauté until tender, but not browned. Add broth and chicken and simmer for 15 minutes. Add salt and pepper to taste and tomato and simmer for 10 minutes longer, then stir in lime juice. Let simmer for 5 more minutes. Add more lime juice if desired. Place tortilla strips in bowls before ladling soup. Place slices of lime on top of soup to garnish.

❖─────────────────❖─────────────────❖

SOPA DE CALABACITAS
ZUCCHINI SOUP

A vegetable soup with a distinct flavor sure to please even the most discerning palate. Can be served either hot or cold.

INGREDIENTS:

4 zucchini
2 cups water
1 cup chicken broth
2 tablespoons parsley leaves
2 tablespoons butter
1 13-oz can evaporated milk

1 tablespoon onion, finely
chopped
1 tablespoon flour
Parsley leaves for garnish
Salt
Pepper

Cut zucchini into large pieces, make sure to wash and cut stems first. Put zucchini and water in a large pan. Bring to a boil. Cover pan and simmer for 15 to 20 minutes. Take pan off heat and cool. Strain zucchini, keep cooking liquid. Put zucchini, 2 tablespoons parsley and 1 cup cooking liquid into a blender and purée. Sauté onion in 2 tablespoons butter until tender, stir in four and cook for 1 minute, stirring. Stir in pureed zucchini, evaporated milk, chicken broth and salt. Cook on medium heat, stir until mixture boils. Garnish with parsley leaves. Served hot or cold. Serves 6.

SOPA DE PESCADO
FISH SOUP

From the bounty of the sea comes this fragrant and flavorful soup that makes a nice light meal when served with tortillas.

INGREDIENTS:

2 fish heads	4 tomatoes
1 1/2 lbs white fish fillets,	1 dried hot chile
cut into chunks	3 tablespoons olive oil
5 cups water	Salt
1 onion	Pepper
2 cloves garlic	Parsley to garnish

Wash fish heads. Fill large pot with water, add fish heads and salt and bring to a boil. Once mixture comes to a boil, reduce heat and simmer for 30 minutes. Remove fish heads and discard. Strain broth and reserve. In a heavy skillet, place tomatoes, onion, chile and garlic cloves and toast lightly over medium heat. When garlic cloves start to brown, remove from skillet. Watch chile to ensure it does not burn, when chile starts turning brown, remove from skillet. Cook tomatoes and onion until scorched on all sides. Peel garlic and scorched tomatoes. Purée scorched onion, chile, garlic and tomatoes in a food processor or blender. Heat olive oil in skillet and add purée. Stir and cook for 5 to 10 minutes over medium heat. Stir together fish broth and purée, bring to a boil. Add fish chunks and bring to a boil, reducing heat once it comes to a boil. Stir and simmer for 10 minutes. Salt and pepper to taste. Garnish with parsley. Serves 6.

❖————————————————❖————————————————❖

SOPA DE TOMATE Y HABA
TOMATO AND LIMA BEAN SOUP

A Mexican favorite with a little something extra. Quite popular while watching bull fights and soccer games.

INGREDIENTS:

1 1-pound package lima beans	2 small yellow onions, peeled
1 sprig parsley	and sliced
3 quarts water	1 chili pequin, crushed
1/4 pound salt pork	Salt
2 large tomatoes, washed and	Croutons
cored	

Soak beans for 3 1/2 hours in 1 1/2 quarts water. Drain and rinse. Place in large pot and cover with remaining 1 1/2 quarts water. Add parsley, salt pork, tomatoes, onions and pequin and salt to taste. Simmer uncovered for 1 hour. Garnish with croutons. Serves 6.

CHILE MENUDO
PEPPER TRIPE STEW

A different twist to a traditional Mexican dish. The addition of red chiles gives this dish its spicy flavor.

INGREDIENTS:

2 pounds tripe, cut into 1 inch
squares
2 gallons water
1 tablespoon salt
1 cup green onion, sliced

1/2 hot red chile pepper, ground
2 green peppers, sliced with seeds
1/3 cup parsley
2 tomatoes, cut in half
Salt

Place tripe in large pot and cover with 1 gallon of water. Bring to a boil. Mix 1 gallon of water with salt and bring to a boil. Drain tripe and cover with salty water. Keep on low boil for 2 hours. Add green onion, chile pepper, green peppers and parsley. Simmer for 1 1/2 hours on low heat. Add tomatoes and simmer for another 30 minutes. Serves 8.

❖————————————————❖————————————————❖

SOPA DE DOROTHY
DOROTHY'S DELIGHTFUL DUMPLING SOUP

A personal favorite of mine, this dish makes a wonderful meal for those cozy evenings in front of a fire.

INGREDIENTS:

3/4 cups flour, sifted
1 teaspoon baking powder
3 large eggs
1/4 cup butter
2 tablespoons grated cheese

4 quarts chicken broth, seasoned
1/2 cup tomato sauce
Parsley
Salt
Pepper

Melt butter and add flour and baking powder. Mix well and add eggs, one at a time, beating well after each egg. Add grated cheese. Heat broth and add tomato sauce. Bring to a boil and drop spoonfuls of dumpling mixture into pot. Cover pan well and simmer for 10 minutes without lifting cover. Garnish with parsley. Serves eight.

❖————————————————❖————————————————❖

SOPA DE ALMEJA MEXICANA
MEXICAN CLAM SOUP

Mexico's coast provides a bountiful selection of fresh seafood. This recipe seems to be a traditional favorite of any coastal community.

INGREDIENTS:

2 cans clams, reserve juice
1 medium onion, diced
1/2 teaspoon garlic powder
4 tablespoons olive oil

1/2 cup tomato sauce
1 Sprig parsley, minced
Salt
Pepper

Sauté onion in oil and add parsley, tomato sauce and garlic powder. Add clams and juice, season with salt and pepper. Heat thoroughly. Serves 4.

ALBONDIGAS
MEATBALL SOUP

Perhaps the most famous of all Mexican soups, this hearty soup is a meal in itself and can easily stand alone as a main course.

INGREDIENTS:

1 medium onion, minced
1/4 teaspoon garlic powder
1/2 can tomato sauce
2 tablespoons oil
3 quarts beef stock
3/4 pound ground beef

3/4 pound ground pork
1/3 cup uncooked rice
2 teaspoons salt
1/2 teaspoon pepper
1 egg, beaten
Sprig of mint, diced

Sauté onion in oil, add garlic powder and mix gently. Add tomato sauce and beef stock. Bring to a boil. Mix meat with egg, rice, mint, salt and pepper and shape into small balls. Drop balls into boiling broth and cover tightly. Cook for 30 minutes. Serves 8.

SOPA DE ELOTE
CORN SOUP

A favorite with Mexican families since the 1500s.

INGREDIENTS:

4 cups corn, fresh is best but
frozen corn, thawed, will work
1 cup chicken stock
1/4 cup butter
4 cups milk

1/2 cup green onion, chopped
6 tablespoons sour cream
3 tablespoons green chilies,
chopped
Salt and pepper

Blend corn and chicken stock to smooth purée. Melt butter and add green onions. Cook until tender and add corn purée. Cook over medium heat for 8 minutes or until thickened. Add milk and salt and pepper to taste. Cook on low for 10 minutes. Ladle soup into bowls and garnish with spoonful of sour cream and chilies and sprinkle chips over top. Serves 6.

MENUDO
TRIPE SOUP

The traditional soup for the morning after, Menudo is a delicious and hearty meal in addition to a tried and true cure for having too much fun.

INGREDIENTS:

2 calves' feet
5 pounds tripe, fresh or pickled
3 cups canned hominy
4 quarts water

2 medium onions, minced
4 cloves garlic, minced
1 1/2 tablespoons salt
1 tablespoon oregano

Wash calves' feet thoroughly. Cool in 4 quarts of water for 1 1/2 hours and cut into small pieces. Wash tripe and cut into small pieces and add to calves' feet. Add onion, garlic, oregano and salt. Simmer on low heat for 4 hours. Add hominy and simmer for 2 1/2 hours. Serves 16.

❖———————————————❖———————————————❖

ESTOFADO A LA MEXICANA
MEXICAN STEW

A tender beef stew that whets your taste buds and sticks to your ribs. A special treat for anyone with a hearty appetite.

INGREDIENTS:

2 pounds beef shank
3 quarts water
3/4 teaspoon garlic powder
1 medium onion, sliced
10 peppercorns
6 tablespoons tomato puree
2 large potatoes, peeled and cubed

3 ears of corn, cut in 1 inch pieces
3 cups green beans, cut into 1 inch pieces
4 medium zucchini, sliced
3 large carrots, peeled and cut in 1 inch pieces
1 tablespoon salt

Brown shanks in a 450°F oven. Combine browned beef, drippings, water, garlic powder, peppercorns, onion and salt in a large pot. Bring to a boil. Cover and cook on low for 2 hours, or until meat is tender. Remove meat. Strain broth and return to pot. Add tomato purée and bring to a boil. Add vegetables and cook on low for 30 minutes or until vegetables are tender. Remove meat from bone and add to soup. Cook long enough to heat meat and serve. Serves 8.

❖———————————————❖———————————————❖

ESTOFADO DE CHILE VERDE
GREEN CHILE STEW

The unique flavor of this spicy stew makes this a Mexican favorite. Makes a meal in itself when served over Mexican rice and with corn tortillas.

INGREDIENTS:

2 pounds boneless pork butt
1 medium onion, chopped
1 clove garlic, minced
2 teaspoons flour
1 8 1/4 ounce can whole tomatoes

1 7-oz. can chopped green chiles
1 10-ounce can tomatoes with hot green chiles
Salt and pepper to taste

Trim fat from pork butt and cut into 1 inch cubes. In a large skillet, brown pork and add onion and garlic. Cook until tender and stir in flour. Cook for 2 minutes, stirring. Add whole tomatoes, chiles and tomatoes with hot chiles. Cut up tomatoes with a fork and continue stirring. Salt and pepper to taste. Simmer on low for 1 to 2 hours, or until meat is tender. Garnish with parsley. Serves 4.

❖————————————————❖————————————————❖

ESTOFADO DE CARNERO Y CHILE
LAMB AND CHILI STEW

This hearty and flavorful stew makes a meal all by itself. Served with warm buttered tortillas and an ice cold cerveza, this is a crowd pleaser.

INGREDIENTS:

2 pounds lamb, cut in chunks
1 onion, sliced
2 tablespoons oil
1/8 teaspoon garlic powder
1 celery stalk, chopped
1 16-oz. canned plum tomatoes, drained

1 1/2 cups corn, fresh or frozen
1 4-ounce can green chilies, drained and chopped
1 cup Mexican beer
1 teaspoon oregano
1/2 teaspoon cumin
Salt and pepper

Cook lamb cubes in oil, browning on all sides. Remove lamb from pan, reserving oils. Add onion, garlic powder, celery and salt and pepper to taste in reserved oil. Cook until tender. Mix in tomatoes, corn, chiles, beer, oregano, cumin and lamb, stirring often. Bring to a boil. Cover and simmer on medium-low heat for 1 3/4 hours, until meat is tender. Serves 6.

❖————————————————❖————————————————❖

A WORD ABOUT PREPARING BROTHS:

Broths, the base stock of many Mexican soups, stews and main dishes, are extremely important to successful Mexican cooking. Chicken broth is made by boiling chicken parts in 3 to 6 quarts of water. Add onion, garlic and salt and pepper to taste. Simmer for 1 1/2 hours. Skim off the excess fat and strain broth. Serve chicken and vegetables and reserve broth for future use. Beef broth is made by boiling beef bones in 3 to 6 quarts of water, add onion, salt, pepper and garlic to taste. Simmer for up to 2 hours. Skim excess fat and strain broth. Broths can be frozen or refrigerated for later use.

ENSALADA DE NOCHE BUENA
CHRISTMAS EVE SALAD

This colorful salad is traditionally served in Mexican households on Christmas Eve. This would be a lovely tradition for your family.

INGREDIENTS FOR THE DRESSING:

1/4 cup white vinegar
3 tablespoons orange juice
1 tablespoon lime juice
1 teaspoon salt
1 teaspoon sugar

1 clove garlic
1/4 teaspoon paprika
1/8 teaspoon white pepper
2/3 cup vegetable oil
3/4 cup pine nuts

INGREDIENTS FOR THE SALAD:

3 oranges, peeled
3 limes, ends discarded and the centers sliced thin and quartered
3 carrots, peeled, cut into 1/4 x 2 inch julienne, blanched 1 minute and chilled
2 ripe bananas, halved lengthwise, slice and sprinkled with lime juice

1 jicama, peel and cut in 1/4 x 2 inch julienne
5 large beets, cooked, chilled and cut into 1/4 x 2 inch julienne
1 romaine lettuce head, cut crosswise into 2 inch thick slices
1/2 fresh pineapple, cut in 1/4 x 2 inch strips

To prepare dressing: Mince garlic in processor. Blend in vinegar, orange and lime juice, salt sugar, paprika and pepper. Keep machine running, add oil in steady stream and mix until creamy. Heat 2 tablespoons dressing in medium skillet on medium-high heat. Add nuts and sauté until golden. Drain nuts on paper towels to absorb excess oil. Combine oranges, limes, carrots, bananas and jicama in large bowl. Pour 2/3 of dressing over top and toss gently to coat. Add remaining dressing to beets and toss. To arrange, line platter with lettuce slices. Arrange beets pinwheel style in center of platter. Mound fruit and vegetables around beets to create a lovely salad. Garnish with pineapple slices. Serves 8.

❖ ━━━━━━━━━━ ❖ ━━━━━━━━━━ ❖

ENSALADA DE CEBOLLA Y NARANJA
ORANGE AND ONION SALAD

INGREDIENTS:

2 red onions, cut into rings
1 large orange, cut in chunks
1 can tangerine slices, drained
1 cup sunflower seeds

1 head lettuce, shredded
Cucumber and melon salsa (see recipe page 20)

In a large salad bowl toss onions, orange, tangerine, sunflower seeds and lettuce. Top with salsa. Serves 4.

Ensalada de Noche Buena, Christmas Eve Salad

ENSALADA DE CINCO FRIJOLES
FIVE BEAN SALAD

This cool and tasty salad is easy to make and goes well with even the hottest Mexican dishes.

INGREDIENTS:

1 cup canned cooked pinto beans, drained
1 cup drained canned black beans
1 8 3/4-ounce can garbanzo beans, drained
1 8-ounce can cut green beans, drained
1 cup canned wax beans, drained
1/2 green pepper, cut in thin strips

1/4 red onion, sliced thin
6 tablespoons oil
3 tablespoons vinegar
1/2 teaspoon salt
1/4 teaspoon oregano
1/8 teaspoon garlic salt
1 tomato, chopped and drained
3 tablespoons mayonnaise
Fresh ground pepper

Combine pinto beans, black beans, green beans, garbanzo beans and wax beans in a large serving bowl. Add red onion and green pepper. Mix together in a small bowl, oil, vinegar, salt, oregano, garlic salt and black pepper to taste. Pour over bean salad and toss gently. Cover and refrigerate overnight. Before serving, add tomato and mayonnaise. Toss to blend.

❖————————❖————————❖

QUELITES CON CHILES
GREENS WITH CHILES

A spicy green salad, perfect with spinach, mustard or swiss chard.

INGREDIENTS:

1 4-ounce can green chiles, drained
1 1/2-pounds fresh greens, spinach, mustard, or swiss chard

2 tablespoons butter
1/2 cup onion, chopped
1 clove garlic, minced
Salt and pepper

Wash greens well. Cook in a small amount of boiling salted water until tender. Drain and chop. Return to saucepan. Melt butter in a small skillet. Add chiles, onion, and garlic and cook until onion is soft, about 5 minutes. Stir chile mixture into chopped greens. Salt and pepper to taste. Heat thoroughly. Serves 6.

❖————————❖————————❖

TOMATILLOS ENSEMA DE ESPARRAGOS
TOMATILLOS OVER ASPARAGUS

This dish combines two popular vegetables to make a colorful and cool salad.

INGREDIENTS:

4 large tomatillos, husked, cored
and chopped fine
1 pound asparagus
1 small tomato, chopped fine

1/2 cup Parmesan cheese
3 tablespoons olive oil
Salt
Pepper

Rinse asparagus and remove tough ends. In a shallow pan, bring 1 inch of water to a boil. Add asparagus and cook for about 4 minutes, until tender. Drain and place in ice water to cool. Drain and arrange asparagus on a platter. Mix tomatillos, tomato and oil. Spoon over asparagus and salt and pepper to taste. Garnish with cheese and serve. Serves 4.

❖————————————————❖   ————————————————❖

ENSALADA DE FRIJOLE VERDE
GREEN BEAN SALAD

This cool and tasty salad is easy to make and goes well with even the hottest Mexican dishes.

INGREDIENTS:

1 pound fresh green beans
1/3 cup olive oil
2 tablespoons lemon juice
Boiling salted water

2 cups water
1/2 medium red onion, sliced thin
1/2 teaspoon oregano
Salt and pepper

Wash green beans and snap off tips. Cut beans in diagonal slices. Cook beans in 1 quart of boiling salted water for 8 minutes, or until tender. Pour beans into a sieve and rinse well in cold water. Drain. Beat olive oil and lemon juice in a small bowl. Pour over beans and add salt and pepper to taste. Toss well. Bring 2 cups water to a boil in a small pan. Slide sliced onions into water and stir. Drain immediately. Place onion slices over beans. Chill. Garnish with oregano. Serves 6.

❖————————————————❖————————————————❖

ENSALADA DE FRIJOLES DE LIMA MEXICANA
MEXICAN LIMA BEANS

A zesty lima bean recipe perfect as a salad or side dish for any meal.

INGREDIENTS:

2 20-ounce packages of frozen
lima beans
2 tablespoons butter

1/2 cup onion, chopped
1 hard boiled egg, chopped
Salt and pepper

Cook beans as directed on package, until tender. Sauté onion and garlic until onion is tender. Stir in tomatoes and chill. Salt and pepper to taste. Drain beans. Pour tomato sauce over beans and stir gently until mixed thoroughly. Garnish with hard boiled egg. Serves 6.

ENSALADA DE COLIFLOR A LA ESPAÑOLA
CAULIFLOWER SALAD, SPANISH STYLE

This is a great make-ahead salad because it needs to be refrigerated for several hours anyway. It also looks very appealing on the plate.

INGREDIENTS:

1/2 cup ripe olives,
2 cups cauliflower (about 1/2 head), sliced
1/3 cup green pepper, chopped

1/4 cup pimiento, chopped
1/4 small onion, chopped
Oil and wine vinegar dressing
1/2 head lettuce

Cut olives into small wedges. Mix with cauliflower, green pepper, onion, pimiento and salt to taste. Mix lightly with oil and wine vinegar dressing. Place in refrigerator for 3 hours. Toss gently before serving and place on lettuce leaves. Serves 6.

❖————————————❖————————————❖

ENSALADA DE CAMARON
SHRIMP SALAD

Hard boiled eggs and shrimp are two of my favorite foods. Try this for a hot summer day, serve with corn tortillas.

INGREDIENTS:

5 hard boiled eggs, shelled
2 cups shrimp, canned or cooked
2 potatoes, cooked
1/4 cup mayonnaise

3 tablespoons wine vinegar
1/4 cup sour cream
1/2 teaspoon chili powder
Salt
Pepper

Chop 2 eggs and cut potatoes in small squares, mix with shrimp. Add 2 tablespoons vinegar and chill for several hours. Shortly before serving, blend mayonnaise, sour cream and salt and pepper to taste. Add chili powder and remaining vinegar and add to shrimp mixture. Place in an attractive serving bowl. Slice remaining eggs and place over the top of the salad. Serves 6.

❖————————————❖————————————❖

PIMIENTOS MORRONES
STUFFED PIMIENTOS

Once you introduce these different looking, but incredibly tasty treats, to your family, and they brave the initial impulse not to try something different, you will have requests to serve them again and again.

INGREDIENTS:

2 cans whole pimientos
2 tablespoons lemon juice
1 5-ounce can chicken
3 hard-boiled eggs, chopped
1 tablespoon onion, minced

1 head of lettuce
Oil and wine vinegar dressing
2 tablespoon parmesan cheese
Salt
Pepper

Place pimientos and their liquid in a medium bowl. Add lemon juice and set aside for at least 3 hours. Mix shredded chicken with its juice with eggs, and onion, mixing well. Drain pimientos and stuff with chicken mixture. Combine pimiento and lime juice with oil and vinegar dressing. Shred lettuce and place on a serving platter. Arrange stuffed pimientos over lettuce and pour dressing over the top. Top with parmesan Serves 6.

❖ ——————————— ❖ ——————————— ❖

ENSALADA VERDE
TOSSED GREEN SALAD

The chili powder and other seasonings give this salad a real spark of flavor. Who would ever think to add so many seasoning?

INGREDIENTS:

1 cup mushrooms, sliced
1 cup cauliflower, separated
1 cup zucchini, sliced
1 small turnip, grated
1/2 cucumber, sliced
1/2 onion, sliced
1/2 piece of celery, chopped
10 olives, sliced
1/4 cup Cheddar cheese, shredded
1/4 cup Monterey Jack Cheese, shredded
1/2 cup sour cream

4 hard boiled eggs, sliced
1 teaspoon cider vinegar
1/2 cup mayonnaise
1/2 teaspoon chili powder
1/2 teaspoon salt
1/2 teaspoon pepper
1/2 teaspoon garlic powder
1/2 teaspoon celery seed
1/2 teaspoon paprika
1/2 teaspoon cilantro
1/2 teaspoon red hot chili seeds
2 tablespoons sunflower seeds

In a very large salad bowl, combine mushrooms, cauliflower, zucchini, shredded turnip, cucumber, onion, celery, olives, and hard boiled eggs. Place bowl in the refrigerator until ready to serve. In a small mixing bowl, blend sour cream, cider vinegar, mayonnaise, chili powder, salt, pepper, garlic powder, celery seed, paprika, cilantro, red hot chili seeds and mix well. When ready to serve salad, pour dressing over the top and garnish with shredded cheese and sunflower seeds, or serve dressing on the side.

❖ ——————————— ❖ ——————————— ❖

A WORD ABOUT SALADS:

For a quick, easy salad, peel a ripe tomato or bell pepper and stuff it with Guacamole (see recipe page 10) or Salsa de Pepino y Melon, cucumber and melon sauce (see recipe page 20).

TOPOPO
MEXICAN CHEF'S SALAD

This recipe combines common ingredients used in many Mexican dishes; beans, tortillas, chiles, cheeses and fresh vegetables. What a combination!

INGREDIENTS:

2 corn tortillas, fried crisp (see recipe on page 42)
1/2 cup refried beans, heated (see recipe page 80)
1 cup sliced turkey
1 medium avocado, peeled, pitted and sliced lengthwise
1/3 cup Cheddar cheese, shredded
1 canned green chile, seeded and chopped

1/4 cup Romano cheese, grated
2 medium tomatoes, cut in wedges
1 teaspoon jalapeño chile, minced
1/2 cup green onion, chopped
2 cup cooked peas, cold
5 cups shredded lettuce
1/4 cup oil
2 tablespoons lemon juice
Salt
Pepper

To make the lettuce layer, mix peas with jalapeno chile, green onion, oil, lettuce, vinegar and salt and pepper to taste. Spread beans over tortillas. Place bean-coated tortillas on separate plates and place a mound of chef's lettuce layer in the center of each tortilla. Place strips of turkey around sides of lettuce. Fill in empty spaces with slices of avocado and spread shredded cheese and chiles over top. Garnish with Romano cheese and tomato wedges. Serves 2.

❖⸺⸺⸺⸺⸺❖⸺⸺⸺⸺⸺❖

ENSALADA DE AGUACATE Y MARISCOS
WARM SCALLOP AND AVOCADO SALAD

It is not a surprise that with such a large coastline, Mexicans love seafood. This dish is a perfect example of the uniqueness and diversity of the Mexican diet.

INGREDIENTS:

2 cups chicken broth
1/3 pound fresh sea scallops
1/4 cup olive oil
1 1/2 tablespoon Dijon mustard

8 large spinach leaves, stemmed
1 medium avocado, peeled, pitted and thinly sliced
Salt and pepper to taste

Heat broth to a low simmer in medium saucepan. Add scallops and poach until opaque, about 2 to 3 minutes. Do not overcook or scallops will be tough. Chill scallops in broth by setting pan in bowl of ice water for about 30 minutes. Slice cooled scallops thin. Combine oil, vinegar, mustard, salt and pepper in a small saucepan and simmer gently. Stack spinach leaves and roll up lengthwise. Cut crosswise. Divide spinach between 2 heated plates. Arrange scallops and avocado decoratively on spinach. Pour warm dressing over salads and serve immediately. Serves 2.

ENSALADA DE PAPAYA CON AGUACATE
PAPAYA AND AVOCADO SALAD

Here we combine the cool, fruity flavor of papayas with the creamy taste of avocados which are a nutritious and a popular ingredient.

INGREDIENTS:

1 head of lettuce
1 ripe papaya, peeled and sliced
2 ripe avocados, peeled and sliced

1/4 cup lime juice
1/4 cup olive oil
Salt and pepper to taste

Divide lettuce and place over six salad plates. Place papaya and avocado slices in alternating layers, or in any decorative design, over lettuce. Combine lime juice, olive oil and salt and pepper to taste and pour over papaya and avocado layers, Serves 6.

❖————————❖————————❖

CALABACITA
ZUCCHINI WITH CORN AND PEPPERS

This bright combination of vegetables will enhance even the most basic meal. Serve as a side to any beef or pork dish.

INGREDIENTS:

3 tablespoons butter
2 pounds zucchini, cubed
1 10-ounce package frozen corn, thawed
1 medium onion, chopped

1 red bell pepper, seeded and chopped
1/4 teaspoon garlic powder
1/2 teaspoon salt
1/2 teaspoon pepper

In a large skillet, melt butter over high heat. Before butter turns brown, add zucchini, corn, onion, bell pepper and garlic powder. Stirring continuously, cook for about 5 minutes. Vegetables should be cooked but still crisp. Add salt and pepper and serve. Serves 8.

❖————————❖————————❖

CUSCURRO DE AJO
GARLIC CROUTONS

Croutons are a great way to use stale bread to make a versatile garnish item.

INGREDIENTS:

1 loaf day old bread
1/2 cup butter or margarine
1/4 cup olive oil

3/4 teaspoon garlic powder
2 tablespoons dried parsley flakes
Salt and pepper to taste

Cut bread into 1 inch cubes and spread evenly over baking sheet. Let dry until bread looses all moisture. In a large skillet heat butter and oil until melted. Add salt, parsley flakes and garlic powder, mix and set aside. Place croutons into large mixing bowl and pour butter mixture over croutons. Stir. Fry until slightly brown. Cool and store in an airtight container.

TORTILLAS Y TAMALES

C orn, an important ingredient in Mexican cooking, was a major part of the diets of prehistoric Indian cultures of the Southwest and Mexico and evidence of its cultivation predates the birth of Christ. Many Mexican dishes enjoyed today are several centuries old.

Tortillas are a versatile food seldom wasted in Mexican kitchens. Leftover tortillas are cut into strips to make *totopos* (corn chips) or *Chilaquiles con Salsa Verde* (Tortilla Strips with Green Sauce). There are two basic types of tortillas, corn and flour. Tortillas may be fried to create crisp shells, steamed to create soft tacos and baked to create an almost endless array of dishes.

❖————————————❖————————————❖

ENCHILADAS PLANAS
FLAT ENCHILADAS

A favorite of both Norte-Americanos and Mexicans, these ground beef enchiladas are popular with the whole family.

INGREDIENTS:

1/2 cup dried pinto beans	2 cups mild Cheddar cheese,
1 medium onion, quartered	shredded
2 cloves garlic	1/2 cup oil
1/2 teaspoon salt	12 corn tortillas
1 1lb 3 oz can enchilada sauce	1 avocado, sliced thin
2 tablespoons oil	3/4 cup sour cream
1 pound ground beef	4 cups lettuce, shredded
1/2 teaspoon oregano	12 ripe olives, pitted
1/2 teaspoon cumin	2 tomatoes, cut in thin wedges

Rinse beans and cover with hot water. Let stand overnight. Drain and rinse well. Add 1/8 onion and 1 clove garlic. Cover with water and bring to a boil. Cover pot and let simmer at low heat for 2 hours. Add 1/2 teaspoon salt and simmer for 2 hours, or until beans are tender. Heat enchilada sauce. Chop remaining onion, mince last clove garlic. Scramble and cook ground beef until light brown. Add onion and garlic. Cook until onion is tender. Add 1 1/4 cups enchilada sauce, oregano and cumin. Add beans and simmer on low for 5 minutes. Add salt to taste. Prepare enchiladas on ovenproof plate. Divide cheese into 4 servings. Preheat oven to 350°F. In heated oil, soften a tortilla for 3 or 4 seconds, turn to cook evenly. Drain on paper towels to absorb extra oil. Place on plate and cover with 1/3 cup meat mixture and a little cheese. Repeat process until there are 3 layers of tortillas, meat and cheese. Cover top layer with 1/4 cup enchilada sauce. Prepare 3 more enchiladas. Bake enchiladas 10 minutes or until cheese is melted. Arrange avocado slices and tomato wedges in circular pattern on top of enchiladas. Top with a dollop of sour cream and an olive. Serves 4.

Enchiladas de Queso, Mexican rice and Guacamole.

TAMALES DE BIANCA
BIANCA'S TAMALES

A traditional holiday favorite in many Mexican homes, tamales are a perfect banquet food for any occasion.

INGREDIENTS:

3 1/2 dozen large dry corn husks
1 cup lard
4 cups masa flour, masa harina
2 teaspoons salt

2 1/2 to 3 cups warm meat or poultry stock for filling (see pages 50-51)

Wash corn husks in warm water, put into a pan and cover with boiling water. Soak for 30 minutes before using. Beat lard until light and fluffy, using a mixer. Gradually beat in masa flour and stock until dough sticks together and has a pastelike consistency. Taste dough before adding salt. If stock is salty you will not need all 2 teaspoons of salt. Dry corn husks by placing on a paper towel and patting dry. Spread about 2 tablespoons tamale dough on center portion of husk, leaving at least a 2 inch margin at both ends and about 1/2 inch margin at right side. Spoon 1 1/2 tablespoons filling onto dough. Wrap tamale, overlapping left side first, then right side slightly over left. Fold bottom up and top down. Lay tamales in top section of steamer with open flaps on bottom. Tie with a string if husks are too short to stay closed. Tamales may completely fill top section of steamer but should be placed so there are spaces between them for circulation of steam. Steam over simmering water for 1 hour, or until corn husk can be peeled from dough easily. Makes 3 1/2 dozen.

❖————————————❖————————————❖

PREPARACION DE TORTILLAS
HOW TO MAKE TORTILLAS

Although the quality of store-bought tortillas is acceptable, nothing beats the freshness of home-made tortillas.

INGREDIENTS FOR CORN TORTILLAS:

2 cups masa harina

1 1/2 cups warm water

Mix masa with warm water to make dough to hold. Shape dough into a ball and divide into 12 pieces. Roll pieces into balls. Place a flattened ball of dough between layers of dampened cheese cloth. Roll with light strokes until dough is about 6 inches around. Pull back cloth carefully and trim to make round. Place tortilla on a sheet of waxed paper and layer paper between each tortilla. To cook, peel off top layer of waxed paper. Place tortilla, paper side up, on an ungreased griddle or frying pan, preheated to medium. Peel off remaining paper as tortilla warms. Cook 1 to 2 minutes, turning often. Tortilla is done when it looks dry and is flecked with light brown spots. Can be reheated. Makes 1 dozen 6 inch tortillas.

INGREDIENTS FOR FLOUR TORTILLAS:

4 cups flour
1/2 cup shortening

1 cup warm water
2 teaspoons salt

Sift four and salt and add shortening. Mix well. Add warm water and mix again. On a lightly floured board, knead about 50 times. Divide dough into 12 even balls and cover with a cloth. Let sit for 15 minutes. Roll each ball into an 8 inch tortilla. Cook on a hot ungreased skillet, turning once, until lightly brown in spots. Do not break air bubbles. Makes 12 tortillas.

TO REHEAT TORTILLAS:

To soften a single tortilla, place tortilla on an ungreased warm griddle or frying pan. Turn often until soft, about 30 seconds. To reheat a package of tortillas in a microwave oven, poke holes in package and microwave for 1 minute.

TO FRY AND FOLD TORTILLAS:

Heat 1/2 inch oil in a frying pan over medium-high heat. When oil is hot, fry one tortilla at a time until tortilla becomes soft. Fold tortilla in half and hold slightly open with tongs to make U shaped. Fry until crisp and lay on paper towel to drain excess oil.

❖————————————————————❖————————————————————❖

ENCHILADAS DE POLLO
CHICKEN ENCHILADAS

A favorite dish of both Norte Americanos and Mexicans, these Chicken Enchiladas are easy to make and perfect for unexpected guests.

INGREDIENTS:

3 cups cooked chicken, chopped
1 7-ounce can green chili salsa
1 4-oz. can chopped green chilies
2 1/2 cups heavy cream
1/2 cup Jack or Colby cheese

12 corn tortillas
3/4 teaspoon salt
2 cups shredded lettuce
12 ripe olives

Mix in a large bowl chicken, chiles and chile salsa. In a separate bowl mix the cream and salt. Soften the corn tortillas by dipping in a pan of heated oil and place tortillas on paper towels to absorb extra oil. Dip each tortilla into the cream mixture before filling with the chicken mixture and rolling. Place filled tortillas in an ungreased baking dish and pour extra cream over the enchiladas. Sprinkle grated Jack or Colby cheese and bake uncovered for 25 minutes. Garnish with shredded lettuce and olives.

CAZUELA DE TAMAL
TAMALE CASSEROLE

This casserole, a take off of the more traditional Tamale, is fast and easy to prepare. Served with a side of rice, makes a most enjoyable meal.

INGREDIENTS:

1 medium onion, chopped
1 pound ground beef
2 cups canned tomatoes
2 cups cream corn
1 cup milk
2 tablespoons oil

1 cup cornmeal, uncooked
2 teaspoons salt
1 teaspoon pepper
2 tablespoons chile powder
1/2 pound Monterey Jack cheese, grated

Heat oil in heavy skillet and cook onion until tender. Add ground beef and brown. Add tomatoes, corn, milk, cornmeal, chile powder, salt and pepper and mix well. Spread grated cheese evenly over mixture and cook on stovetop for 25 minutes. Serves 8.

❖ ——————————————— ❖ ——————————————— ❖

PAY DE POLLO ESTILO TAMAL
CHICKEN TAMALE PIE

My elderly friend, Maria, tells of the days she wooed the young men in her village with this traditional dish.

INGREDIENTS FOR FILLING:

1/4 cup lard or cooking oil
1 cup onion, chopped
1 clove garlic, minced
1 16 ounce can cooked tomatoes

1 1/2 teaspoons salt
1 tablespoon chili powder
1/2 teaspoon cumin
3 cups diced cooked chicken

INGREDIENTS FOR TAMALE DOUGH:

1/2 cup lard
3 cups masa flour (masa harina)
1 teaspoon baking powder

1/2 teaspoon salt
1 cup chicken stock

To prepare filling, heat lard in large pan. Add onion and garlic and cook for 5 minutes, or until onion is tender. Add tomatoes and seasonings. Bring tomatoes to a boil. Mix well. Simmer on medium heat for 10 minutes. Stir in chicken and simmer for 5 minutes. To prepare tamale dough, beat lard until light and fluffy, using spoon or mixer. Combine masa flour, baking powder and salt. Gradually beat flour mixture and chicken stock into lard until dough sticks together and has a pastelike consistency. Preheat oven to 350°F. Grease a large casserole dish. Press tamale dough onto bottom and sides of dish in a 1/2 inch layer. Reserve dough to cover top. Pour in prepared filling. Cover filling with remaining dough and pat into a layer the same thickness as the lining. Bake for 1 hour. Serves 6.

PAY DE PUERCO ESTILO TAMAL
PORK TAMALE PIE

This is another original recipe contributed by my friend Maria. She enjoys cooking with white meats.

INGREDIENTS FOR FILLING:

1 1/2 pounds ground pork	1 tablespoon chili powder
1/2 cup onion, chopped	1 1/2 teaspoons salt
2 cups cooked tomatoes	1/2 teaspoon oregano
1 clove garlic	1/4 teaspoon pepper

INGREDIENTS FOR CORNMEAL TOPPING:

1 cup yellow cornmeal	1/2 teaspoon salt
2 tablespoons flour	1 egg
1 tablespoon sugar	1/2 cup milk
2 teaspoons baking powder	1 tablespoon oil

To prepare filling, brown scrambled pork, stirring to cook evenly. Purée onion, 1/2 of the tomatoes, garlic and chili powder in a blender. Gradually add the remaining tomatoes and blend until puréed. Pour tomato purée into a skillet with meat. Bring to a boil. Simmer on low heat. Stir in salt, oregano and pepper. Simmer covered for 30 minutes. To prepare cornmeal topping, mix cornmeal with flour, sugar, baking powder and salt in a bowl. Preheat oven to 425°F. Beat egg slightly. Beat in milk and shortening. Add liquid ingredients to dry ingredients all at once and stir lightly, just until all dry ingredients are moistened. Do not beat. Spoon batter over simmering filling. Bake 20 to 25 minutes, until topping is lightly browned.

❖————————————————❖————————————————❖

ENCHILADAS DE QUESO
CHEESE ENCHILADAS

INGREDIENTS FOR FILLING:

1 cup Cheddar cheese, shredded	6 corn tortillas (see recipe page 42)
2 1/3 cup canned Enchilada Sauce	1 small onion, chopped
1 cup Monterey Jack cheese,	3 green onions, chopped
shredded	1/4 cup oil

Heat enchilada sauce in pan. Mix cheeses and set aside. Fry tortillas, one at a time, in hot oil for 3 to 5 seconds per side. Drain on paper towels and immediately dip in heated sauce. Place tortilla on a plate and spread cheese in a line just below the center. Lightly spread chopped onion over cheese. Roll tortilla tightly and place seam down in a shallow baking dish. Repeat with each tortilla, saving 1/3 of the cheese to use as topping. When all enchiladas are prepared, cover with left over sauce and top with cheese. Bake 15 to 20 minutes. Garnish with green onions and serve hot.

BURRITOS
BEAN FILLED TORTILLAS

A quiick and easy snack food and a great alternative to the basic peanut butter and jelly lunch.

INGREDIENTS:

3 1/2 cups refried beans, (canned or see recipe on page 80)
15 flour tortillas, warmed (see recipe page 43)
1 1/2 cups ground beef filling, (see recipe page 50)

Lay one tortilla on a plate and place 4 tablespoons refried beans in the middle. Spread beans evenly over tortilla, leaving about 1 inch uncovered around edges. Spoon 1 heaping tablespoon beef filling over 1/2 of beans, leaving edges of tortilla uncovered. Sprinkle chopped onion as desired. Fold tortilla by folding sides of tortilla until outer edges meet in the middle. Roll from the bottom of the tortilla until completely rolled. Serve with the seam down. Serves 15.

❖————————————————❖————————————————❖

ENCHILADAS DE QUESO Y CREMA
CREAM CHEESE ENCHILADAS

Most people get glasses when they visit their optometrist, I got this different but savory recipe. Thanks Doc!

INGREDIENTS:

1 5-ounce can cooked chicken
1 4-oz. can green chiles, sliced
1 8-ounce package cream cheese, sliced thin
12 corn tortillas
1 12-ounce can enchilada sauce
2 cups Monterey Jack cheese, shredded
1/4 cup oil

Preheat oven to 350°F. Pour enchilada sauce in a shallow dish. Heat oil in a skillet and cook tortillas for 30 seconds. Remove tortillas from oil and dip in enchilada sauce. Place 2 tablespoons chicken,slice of cream cheese and chiles just off center of tortilla and roll. Place rolled enchiladas in a 9x13" baking dish and pour remaining enchilada sauce over all. Spread shredded cheese on top and bake for 20 minutes, until cheese has melted.

❖————————————————❖————————————————❖

A WORD ABOUT INGREDIENTS:

Corn husks, used in the preparation of tamales, are sold by the package and can be found in Mexican markets and many well-stocked grocery stores in the Southwest. To use, soften by soaking corn husks in warm water for 2 to 3 hours. Discard any miscellaneous pieces of silk.

ENCHILADA A LA CASEROLA
Enchilada Casserole

A perennial favorite of both Norte-Americanos and Mexicans, these Chicken Enchiladas are plumper than most and a perfect banquet food.

INGREDIENTS:

12 corn tortillas (recipe page 42)
3/4 cup oil
6 large green onions, chopped
3 cups enchilada sauce

3 cups Monterey Jack cheese, shredded
1 can pitted ripe olives, cut in quarters

Cut tortillas into quarters. Fry a few at a time in hot oil for 30 seconds. Place on paper towels to absorb excess oil. Preheat oven to 350°F. Set aside 1 tablespoon green onion. Mix remaining green onions with cheese. Spoon enchilada sauce evenly over the bottom of a large casserole dish. Cover sauce with 1/3 of the tortillas. Top with 1/3 of the sauce, making sure to cover all tortillas in sauce. Top with 1/3 of the cheese mixture and olives. Repeat layering ingredients. Bake for 20 minutes, or until cheese is melted. Serves 8.

❖————————————————❖————————————————❖

ENCHILADA A LA VERACRUZANA
Veracruz Enchiladas

The crab filling, with its capers, almonds and raisins, gives this dish its style. This is no run-of-the-mill enchilada!

INGREDIENTS:

1 tablespoon parsley, chopped
1 tablespoon almonds, chopped
1 1 lb 3 oz can enchilada sauce

1/4 cup oil
6 corn tortillas
Sour cream

INGREDIENTS FOR CRAB FILLING:

6 ounces canned crab, drained
1 tablespoon raisins, plumped in hot water, drained
1 tablespoon almonds, chopped
1 tablespoon parsley, chopped

1 tablespoon oil
1 clove garlic, minced
1/2 medium onion, chopped
1 teaspoon capers
Salt and pepper to taste

To prepare crab filling, sauté onion and garlic in hot oil. Add flaked crab, raisins, and capers. Mix well. Cook over medium heat for 4 minutes. Preheat oven to 350°F. Warm enchilada sauce. Fry tortillas, one at a time, in hot oil for 3 to 5 seconds, each side. Drain over paper towels to absorb excess oil. Spoon a generous amount of crab filling on each tortilla. Roll and place in baking dish. After all tortillas are filled and rolled, cover with enchilada sauce. Place foil over baking dish and bake for 15 to 20 minutes. Garnish with sour cream, parsley and almonds. Serves 6.

RELLENO DE CARNE
MEAT FILLINGS

There are many ways to fill tacos, bell peppers, tamales and even whole California chiles. For easy entertaining, prepare fillings in advance and freeze. The filling recipes that follow offer a variety of delightful tastes.

❖————————————————❖————————————————❖

CARNE DESHEBRADA
SHREDDED MEAT

INGREDIENTS:

1/2 medium onion, sliced thin
1 pound beef stew meat
1 tablespoon chili powder
1 clove garlic, minced

1 1/2 cups water
2 tablespoons oil
3 medium tomatoes, peeled and chopped

Combine beef water and salt to taste in large pot. Bring to a boil. Simmer, covered, on low heat for 1 3/4 hours, or until beef is tender. Set aside to cool. Drain and reserve broth. Shred meat with a fork. Sauté onion and garlic until tender. Add tomatoes and simmer for 10 minutes. Stir in green pepper, chili powder and meat. Add 1/2 cup broth and salt and pepper to taste. Simmer on low for 15 minutes, until green pepper is tender.

❖————————————————❖————————————————❖

PUERCO RELLENO
PORK FILLING

INGREDIENTS:

5 pound pork bone-in shoulder
1/2 teaspoon cumin
1/2 teaspoon coriander
1 teaspoon oregano

2 medium onions, chopped
2 carrots, chopped
Water
Salt and Pepper

Cover pork shoulder with water in a large pot. Add salt, cumin, coriander, oregano, onion, and carrots. Bring to a boil and cover. Reduce heat to medium low and simmer for 3 hours. When meat is tender remove from pot and place in a baking pan. Reserve broth for soups. Bake at 350°F for 45 minutes or until meat is very well browned. Drain off all fat and shred meat. Fills 6 enchiladas.

Chicken and Beef Tamales and Bean Burrito

RELLENO DE CARNE MOLIDA
HAMBURGER FILLING

INGREDIENTS:

1 pound ground beef	Salt
1 medium onion, chopped	Pepper
1/2 cup canned enchilada sauce	Oil

Scramble and brown meat, adding oil if necessary. Add onion and cook until tender. Mix in enchilada sauce and simmer, covered, for 15 minutes. Salt and pepper to taste. Fills 6 to 8 tacos.

❖———————————————❖———————————————❖

RELLENO DE CARNE PICADA
MINCED MEAT FILLING

INGREDIENTS:

1/2 pound ground beef	1 medium tomato, peeled and chopped
1/2 pound ground pork	
1/2 small onion, chopped	2 tablespoons blanched almonds, chopped
1/4 teaspoon garlic powder	
2 teaspoons capers	2 tablespoons raisins, soaked in hot water until soft
2 tablespoons parsley	

Cook and scramble beef and pork until light brown. Drain excess oil. Add onion, tomato, garlic, capers, almonds, and raisins. Cook over medium heat for 10 minutes, stirring often. Salt to taste.

❖———————————————❖———————————————❖

RELLENO DE CHORIZO
CHORIZO FILLING

INGREDIENTS:

1 pound ground beef	1/2 teaspoon each salt and pepper
1/2 pound ground pork	1 teaspoon oregano
1 large onion, chopped fine	5 tablespoons vinegar
2 teaspoons chili powder	1 1/2 cups canned enchilada sauce
1/2 teaspoon cumin	

Mix beef, pork, onion, chili powder, cumin, cinnamon, salt, vinegar, and oregano. Fry mixture until pink color becomes brown, skimming excess fat. Add enchilada sauce and bring to a boil. Simmer until mixture reaches desired thickness, adding water if a thinner consistency is desired. Salt and pepper to taste.

POLLO RELLENO
CHICKEN FILLING

INGREDIENTS:

2 cups shredded chicken
2/3 cups canned enchilada sauce
1 small canned jalapeno chile,
chopped

1 medium onion, chopped
1/4 cup raisins
2 tablespoons oil
Salt and pepper

Cook onion in oil until tender, add chicken, enchilada sauce, chile and raisins. Simmer for 10 minutes, stirring often. Salt and pepper to taste.

CANGREJO RELLENO
CRAB FILLING

INGREDIENTS:

6 ounces canned crab, drained
1 tablespoon raisins, plumped in
hot water, drained
1 tablespoon almonds, chopped
1 tablespoon parsley, chopped

1 tablespoon oil
1 clove garlic, minced
1/2 medium onion, chopped
1 teaspoon capers
Salt and pepper to taste

Sauté onion and garlic in hot oil. Add flaked crab, raisins, and capers. Mix well. Cook over medium heat for 4 minutes. Fills 6 tacos or enchiladas.

TACOS
FILLED TORTILLAS

INGREDIENTS:

1 pound ground beef
1 1/2 teaspoons chili powder
1 medium onion, chopped fine
1/2 teaspoon oregano
1/2 teaspoon paprika
1/4 teaspoon garlic salt

2 teaspoons Worcestershire
1/4 teaspoon rosemary
1/4 teaspoon cumin
12 corn tortillas, fried and folded
1 cup Cheddar cheese, shredded
1 head lettuce, shredded

Scramble meat in a skillet and cook until brown. Add onion and chili powder, oregano, paprika, cumin, rosemary, garlic salt, pepper, and Worcestershire sauce. Simmer for 15 minutes on low, stirring occasionally. Fill folded tortilla with taco meat, lettuce, cheese, tomatoes and top with your choice of taco sauce. For a soft taco, spoon filling slightly off center of tortilla and fold. Makes 12 tacos.

CHILE Y ESTOFADO
STEWS AND CHILI

The history of chili is as spicy as the dish itself. Texans have long laid claim to the credit of its creation. For those people who are known as 'chiliheads' there is no finer food and many claim that a good bowl of chili can cure what ails you. Some chili purists believe chili should consist of only a sauce with hunks of beef. Many others feel that a bowl of chili wouldn't be complete without the addition of beans and other vegetables, while still others live by the belief that whatever you may have lying around the kitchen should be thrown into the pot. Whether you're an old 'chilihead' or just a beginner, you will love the selections of chilis we have for you. Also, our selection of the more traditional Mexican stews, or *Estofado,* will be sure to please the non-chili lovers. Enjoy!

❖————————————❖————————————❖

ALBONDIGON CON CHILE
CHILI WITH MEATBALLS

INGREDIENTS:

1/2 pound ground pork
1 pound ground beef
1 green pepper, chopped
2 medium onions, chopped fine
2 tablespoons mild chili powder

1 12-ounce can tomato paste
1 32-ounce canned kidney beans, drained
1 24-oz canned stewed tomatoes
Salt and pepper

In a large saucepan, or skillet, combine stewed tomatoes, onions, green pepper, tomato paste, chili powder and salt and pepper to taste. Bring to a boil. Simmer, covered, for 2 hours, stirring often. Combine beef and pork and make 1 inch balls. Brown meatballs in a separate pan. Drain excess oil and add to tomato mixture. Simmer on low heat for 1 hour. Add beans and cook for 15 minutes. Serves 6.

❖————————————❖————————————❖

CHILE CON CARNE
CHILI WITH MEAT

INGREDIENTS:

2 pounds ground beef
1/2 cup chopped onion
1 1/4 cups canned tomatoes

4 cups canned kidney beans
1 teaspoon sugar
2 tablespoons chili powder

In a large skillet brown beef and add onions, tomatoes, beans, sugar and chili powder. Cover and cook slowly for at least on hour. Top with grated Jack cheese and serve with crackers or tortillas. Serves 8

FRIJOLES BLANCOS CON CHILE
CHILI AND WHITE BEANS

INGREDIENTS:

3 pounds ground beef
1/2 pound dry navy beans, rinsed
6 cups water
1 teaspoon cumin powder
1/2 teaspoon garlic powder

1 bay leaf
2 teaspoons salt
1 teaspoon oregano
2 tablespoons paprika
1 teaspoon brown sugar
1 tablespoon chili powder

Brown ground beef. Add water, bay leaf, garlic powder, salt, oregano, paprika, cumin powder, navy beans, brown sugar and chili powder. Cook over low heat for 3 hours uncovered and one hour covered. Serves 6.

❖————————————————❖————————————————❖

CHILE DE CERVEZA
BEER CHILI

Cooking with beer probably started when a cook had too many cervezas and decided to share one. The alcohol is cooked out but a special flavor remains.

4 pounds ground beef
3 onions, chopped
1 teaspoon cumin powder
1/8 teaspoon garlic powder
1 12 ounce can tomatoes
1 teaspoon sugar

1/2 can Mexican beer
2 packs chili seasoning
1 tablespoon Tabasco sauce
1 quart water
4 jalapeno peppers, chopped
Salt and pepper

Brown ground beef thoroughly. Add onion, cumin powder, garlic powder and salt and pepper to taste. Mix in tomatoes, sugar, beer, chili seasoning, chili powder, Tabasco sauce, water and peppers. Cook on low for 3 hours, uncovered. Serves 8.

❖——— ————————————❖————————————————❖

A WORD ABOUT CHILES:

The Anaheim chile, also called California, is a large mild flavored green or yellow chile. The Poblano chile is a large green chile that can be both mild and very, very hot. It is most often used for Chile Relleno. Jalapeño chiles are small, green or yellow, and so hot you may think your mouth is on fire. When a Jalapeño chile has been smoked and dried it becomes a Chipotle chile which has a wonderfully smoky flavor. The heat comes from the capsaicin oil which is concentrated in the placenta or veins of the chile, the seeds are hot because of their close proximity to the veins.

COMPOTA DE POLLO
STEWED CHICKEN

I love this recipe for its to-die-for flavor. The garlic and vinegar mixture gives the chicken a subtle flavor that tastes wonderful.

INGREDIENTS:

1 3-to-4 pound broiler-fryer
1/8 teaspoon garlic powder
1/2 teaspoon salt
1/8 teaspoon pepper
3 tablespoons white vinegar
3 tablespoons oil

1 medium onion, chopped
3 large tomatoes, peeled and chopped
12 Spanish green olives
1/2 teaspoon oregano
1 teaspoon salt

Cut chicken in quarters, wash and pat dry. Mix garlic with 1/2 teaspoon salt, pepper and vinegar. Rub mixture all over chicken. Let stand for one hour before cooking. Brown chicken quarters in a skillet using 3 table-spoons oil. Place browned chicken in large pot. Add onion, tomatoes, olives, capers, oregano and 1 teaspoon salt. Bring to a boil. Cover and simmer on low heat for 1 hour, turning chicken pieces often. Serves 4.

❖━━━━━━━━━━━━━❖━━━━━━━━━━━━━❖

CHILI DE CALABACITAS
ZUCCHINI CHILI

INGREDIENTS:

1 medium zucchini, chopped
1/4 cup oil
2 pounds ground beef
1 medium onion, chopped
1 small green pepper, chopped
1 teaspoon sugar

2 teaspoons tabasco sauce
1 8-oz can of whole kernel corn
1 16-ounce can pinto beans
2 tablespoons chili powder
1 6-ounce can tomato paste
Salt and Pepper

Sauté chopped zucchini in oil and set aside. Brown ground beef, chopped onion and green pepper. Mix sugar, tabasco sauce, corn, beans, chili powder and tomato paste to browned ground beef and mix. Add cooked zucchini and drippings. Cook on low for 2 hours. Add water until desired thickness is achieved. Serves 4 to 6.

❖━━━━━━━━━━━━━❖━━━━━━━━━━━━━❖

CARNE COCIDOS
BOILED BEEF

This is a hearty beef, bean and vegetable stew that will be sure to satisfy even the biggest appetite. Serve this with a chunk of cornbread.

INGREDIENTS:

4 chicken breasts
1 3-pound chuck roast
2 cups navy beans
3 cups water
1/4 cup olive oil
2 medium onions

4 medium potatoes
4 large carrots
4 medium parsnips
3 peppercorns
Croutons (see page 39)
Salt and pepper

Cover and soak beans overnight. Drain. In a large Dutch Oven, heat oil and add chicken and chuck roast. Fry both until completely brown. Add beans to the Dutch Oven and add enough water to cover meat and beans. Bring to a boil. Simmer for 3 hours. As meat and beans simmer, slice vegetables then add, with spices, to stew. Cook over medium low heat for 1 1/2 hours, or until meat is tender. Remove vegetables and meat from mixture. To serve, pour broth into soup bowls and garnish with croutons. Serve meat and vegetables together. Serves 6.

❖———————————————❖———————————————❖

ESTOFADO CHILE
CHILE STEW

INGREDIENTS:

4 Anaheim chiles, seeded and chopped
3 jalapeño chiles, seeded and sliced
1 pound Italian sausage
1 large onion, chopped
1 clove garlic, minced

4 tomatoes, chopped
1 8-ounce can tomato sauce
1 cup frozen corn
1 cup Cheddar cheese, shredded
1 cup Monterey Jack cheese, shredded
1 teaspoon each salt and pepper

Prepare fresh Anaheim chiles as directed on page 12. Slice or scramble sausage and cook over medium heat. When meat has browned, drain off excess oil. Add onion and garlic and sauté for 4 minutes, or until onion is tender. Add chiles, tomatoes, corn and sauce. Simmer for 45 minutes over medium heat, stirring occasionally. Add 3/4 cup of each cheese and stir until melted. Use extra cheese as garnish. Serves 6.

❖———————————————❖—————— ————❖

A WORD ABOUT TOMATILLOS:

Tomatillos, a small green vegetable, similar to tomatoes but with their own unique flavor, are often used in Mexican cooking. They have an almost sweet flavor that is quite unique. Tomatillos have a dry outer husk-like layer which becomes tan and will start to separate from the body when ripened. Tomatillos will stay fresh for months if stored, with husks intact, in a cool dry place. If tomatillos cannot be found, green tomatoes will do as a replacement.

CHILE A LA RIO GRANDE
RIO GRANDE CHILI

This biggest thing about this chili is the flavor, with eight different spices it will definitely affect your taste buds. Serve with cerveza.

INGREDIENTS:

1 1/2 pounds ground beef
1/2 cup bacon, diced
2 yellow onions, diced
1 1lb 4-oz can red kidney beans
1/2 teaspoon oregano
1 teaspoon ground cumin
1 tablespoon chili powder
1/2 teaspoon Tabasco

1 teaspoon paprika
1 medium hot red pepper, crushed
1/2 teaspoon garlic powder
2 cups canned tomatoes
1/2 teaspoon basil
1 teaspoon salt
Cayenne pepper

Cook bacon in large heavy skillet. Add onions and sauté until tender. Add cumin, oregano, hot red pepper, paprika, Tabasco, chili powder, cayenne pepper, salt and garlic powder and mix well. Add tomatoes and kidney beans and simmer slowly for 1/2 hour stirring occasionally. Add ground chuck and cook for ten minutes on low, stirring occasionally. Serves 8.

❖———————————————❖———————————————❖

PUERCO CON PINA
PORK WITH PINEAPPLE

Out of all the recipes I've tried out on my family, this is my brother-in-laws favorite. He raves about this and I think you will, too.

INGREDIENTS:

3 pound pork loin, cut in chunks
1 large tomato, peeled and chopped
1 cup onion, chopped
1 cup beef stock
1/4 cup dry sherry

1/3 cup sliced pimento
2 cups pineapple chunks, with juice
1/2 teaspoon chili powder
2 tablespoons flour
Salt and pepper to taste

Brown meat in a large skillet until meat is browned on all sides. Add the onion and cook for 5 minutes, or until onion is tender. Add the pineapple with its juice, beef stock, dry sherry, sliced pimento, tomato and chili powder to the skillet. Mix well then bring to boil. Reduce heat and simmer. Add salt and pepper to taste. Cover and simmer for 1 1/2 hours, until meat is tender. Stir often to prevent sticking. Approximately 1/2 hour before serving, sprinkle flour over simmering sauce and stir until sauce thickens. Serve in bowls by itself, or over rice. Serves 8.

Puerco con Pina with peppers

MOLE POBLANO DE GUAJOLOTE
TURKEY MOLE POBLANO

Chicken can be used as a substitution for turkey. However, I find this an excellent way to utilize leftover turkey.

INGREDIENTS:

1 8-ounce jar mole poblano paste	1 cup chicken broth
3 cups diced cooked turkey	Sugar
1 cup canned tomato sauce	Salt

Blend mole paste, tomato sauce and stock in a large pot. Bring to a boil and add sugar and salt to taste. Stir in chicken and simmer on medium low heat for 15 minutes, stirring often to blend flavors. To use as a tamale filling, the sauce must be thick, so simmer until desired consistency. Then spoon turkey pieces and sauce onto tamale dough spread on corn husks. Use left over sauce to serve over cooked tamales. Or Turkey Mole may be served as a stew or over rice. Serves 4.

❖————————————————❖————————————————❖

CHILE DE LA VALLE
VALLEY CHILI

A chili like this does not come along every day. My good friend, Maria, gave me this recipe that is her daughter's favorite.

INGREDIENTS:

4 pounds beef steak, cut in slices	1 tablespoon oregano
2 12-ounce cans tomato sauce	1 tablespoon sugar
1 12-ounce can of water	1 tablespoon pepper
5 large onions, chopped	1 tablespoon salt
2 bell peppers	1/2 teaspoon cilantro
1 can cola drink	1/4 cup oil
9 tablespoons chili powder	

Mix cola with chili powder, sugar, oregano, pepper, salt and cilantro. and set aside. Heat oil in a skillet and sautée onions until tender. Remove to a large pot. Discard excess oil and using the same pan, brown the beef steak. Place the steak in the large pot with onions. Mix the spice mixture with tomato sauce and water and stir into pot. Simmer for 3 hours, stirring often. When meat becomes tender add salt and pepper to taste and place in the refrigerator for 3 hours. Reheat and add lime juice when ready to serve. Serves 6.

❖————————————————❖————————————————❖

A WORD ABOUT PAPRIKA
Paprika is dried ground ripe bell pepper, the mildest of all peppers.

PAELLA
RICE AND SEAFOOD

This dish seems to cross many cultures and boundaries. This is our version of a very traditional repast.

INGREDIENTS:

1 cup rice	1/3 cup carrots, chopped
1/4 cup olive oil	15 mussels, in shells
2 patties chorizo (see recipe 90)	10 clams, in shells
1 cup clam juice	10 raw shrimp, in shells (fresh
1 cup chicken broth	or frozen)
1 cup peas	Saffron

Pour oil and rice into a Dutch Oven, cooking until golden brown. Add chorizo, chicken broth, peas, carrots, clam juice and a dash of saffron to rice and mix well. Drop mussels, clams and shrimp on top of rice and bring to a boil. Simmer for 20 minutes, covered, without lifting cover or stirring. Transfer to a large serving bowl. Serves 8.

❖———————————————❖———————————————❖

CROQUETTA DE CAMARON Y CHILE
SHRIMP PATTIES AND CHILE

Shrimp Patties and Chile can be served as an appetizer, or with side dishes such as rice and beans to make a full meal.

INGREDIENTS:

5 medium potatoes	1 4-ounce package dried shrimp,
1/4 cup evaporated milk	powdered
1 1/2 tablespoons chili powder	1 1/2 cup water
1/8 teaspoon garlic powder	2 eggs, beaten
2 tablespoons flour	Salt
1/4 cup corn oil	Pepper

Boil potatoes until tender. Peel and mash. Add evaporated milk, flour and beaten eggs. Mix in salt and pepper to taste. Stir mixture until smooth. Add powdered shrimp and stir until mixture can be formed into small patties. Fry patties in oil until lightly brown. Set aside. Combine oil, garlic, water, flour and chili powder. Simmer over medium heat for 15 minutes, until sauce is smooth and thick, stirring often. Dip the fried patties in sauce and place on a large dish. Pour remaining hot sauce over patties. Serves 6.

❖———————————————❖———————————————❖

A WORD ABOUT FISH BROTH
For fish broth, follow the recipe on page 27, substituting fish for chicken.

CARNES Y AVES
MEATS AND POULTRY

I n Mexico, meat doesn't always play a large part in the main meal of the day. Tortillas, beans and chiles are staple foods and meats are additions, not always a main focus, to meals. Meat is often shredded and cooked with chiles and other vegetables to stretch it's quantity. Of course, most Norte Americanos rely on a good piece of meat or poultry to round out a meal. Following are recipes that combine the best of two cooking cultures.

❖————————————————❖————————————————❖

LOMO DE PUERCO
BAKED PORK LOIN

No one cooks pork loin like my sister, Dee Linda. This is her favorite recipe.

INGREDIENTS:

1 3 pound pork loin roast
1 tablespoon chili powder
2 cloves garlic

1/2 teaspoon oregano
1 16-ounce bottle of Coca Cola
Salt and pepper to taste

Preheat oven to 350°F. Mix chili powder, garlic, oregano and 1/4 bottle of cola in a blender or food processor. Salt and pepper the pork roast evenly. Brown all sides of pork roast in a skillet. Drain excess oils from meat and put into a baking pan. Spread cola mixture over meat. Add remaining cola to meat and place in preheated oven. Bake for 2 hours, or until a meat thermometer reaches 170°F. Baste often with pan mixture. Serve pan fluid as sauce when serving meat. Serves 6.

❖————————————————❖————————————————❖

POLLO CON CACAHUATE
PEANUT CHICKEN

INGREDIENTS:

1 3-lb chicken fryer, cut in pieces
5 cups water
1/8 teaspoon garlic powder
2 tablespoons mild chili powder

3 tablespoons peanut butter
2 tablespoons oil
1/3 cup sherry
Salt and pepper

Place chicken in a pot with 5 cups water. Add garlic, and salt. Cook until meat is tender and can be picked from bones. Reserve broth and set aside. Combine chili powder, 2 1/2 cups broth, peanut butter and sherry. Stir for 10 minutes, until sauce is smooth. Add chicken to sauce and simmer for 10 minutes, until sauce is medium thick. Serves 5.

Preceding pages: (Clockwise, from left to right) Civiche, Fajitas, Guacamole and Mexican Rice, Black Bean Soup and Chicken Enchiladas.

POLLO CON JOCOQUI
SOUR CREAM CHICKEN

A rich tasting chicken dish perfect for dinner parties. Serve with green rice.

INGREDIENTS:

1 5 lb roasting chicken, pieced	1/2 cup sour cream
1/4 cup chicken broth	1/2 cup heavy cream
1/4 cup butter	2 cups flour
1 medium onion, chopped	1 cup oil
1 clove garlic, crushed	1 1/2 tablespoon salt
3 tablespoons butter	1 1/2 tablespoon pepper

Cook chicken giblets and neck in pot of water to make the broth. Combine flour, salt and pepper. Coat chicken pieces with the seasoned flour and brown in oil, turning to brown evenly. Grease a roasting pan and arrange chicken in pan. Dot with butter and pour broth over the chicken. Bake at 350°F until chicken is tender, approximately 30 minutes. Sauté onion and garlic in 2 tablespoons of butter and discard garlic. Add sour cream, heavy cream and salt and pepper to taste. Heat but do not boil. Place chicken on a platter and pour sauce over chicken. Serves 8.

❖————————————————❖————————————————❖

FAJITAS
VEGETABLES AND STEAK STRIPS

Fajitas are another Texas original along with many other great Tex-Mex recipes. Chicken can be substituted for the steak if you so desire.

INGREDIENTS:

1 3/4 pounds top sirloin steak	1/2 teaspoon garlic salt
1 green pepper, diced	1 8 1/4-oz can stewed tomatoes
1 small onion, chopped	1 teaspoon Worcestershire sauce
1 tablespoon hot pepper sauce	1 teaspoon oregano
2 tablespoons oil	Salt and pepper

Cut meat in 2 x 1/4 inch strips. In a large skillet heat oil over high heat. When the skillet and oil are hot, add beef strips very carefully. Do not splatter oil. Cook until brown, moving meat rapidly to avoid unnecessary charring. When the beef strips are browned to the desired color, reduce heat and add green pepper, hot pepper sauce, onion and garlic salt. Cook until vegetables are tender. Add tomatoes, Worcestershire sauce, oregano and salt and pepper to taste. Simmer on medium for 45 minutes or until most of the juices have evaporated and meat is tender. Serve with flour tortillas, sour cream, guacamole and a side dish of grated cheese.

PICADILLO DE POLLO Y FRUTA
SPICED FRUITY CHICKEN

This is the perfect recipe to turn to when plain old chicken just doesn't do it for you. It is easy to prepare and wonderful to eat.

INGREDIENTS:

2 frying chickens, cut in pieces
1/2 cup crushed pineapple
1 1/2 teaspoons salt
1/4 teaspoon pepper
1/4 teaspoon cinnamon
1/4 teaspoon cloves

2 cloves garlic, minced
1/4 cup oil
1/2 cup onion, chopped
1/2 cup raisins
2 cups orange juice
1/2 cup dry sherry

Combine salt, pepper, cinnamon, cloves, and garlic and mix well. Rub into chicken. In a large skillet, heat oil and brown chicken evenly. Place browned chicken in a large pot. Saute onion in remaining oil in skillet. Add onion to chicken along with raisins, pineapple and orange juice. Add water, if needed, to cover chicken. Bring to a boil. Cover and simmer over medium heat for 1 hour, until chicken is tender. Add sherry and cook for 5 more minutes. Serves 8.

CHULETA DE PUERCO CON TOMATILLO Y PIMIENTO
TOMATO AND PEPPER PORK CHOPS

This is another very easy to prepare dish that gives the impression of much time spent in the kitchen in preparation.

INGREDIENTS:

6 pork chops
1 tablespoon oil
7 medium tomatoes, chopped

3 green peppers, chopped
2 tablespoons flour
Salt and pepper

Sift the flour, salt and pepper to taste. Coat pork chops with flour mixture and brown in a skillet. Add tomatoes and peppers and cover. Simmer for 25 minutes. Serves 6.

A WORD ABOUT MEXICAN MEALS:

In Mexico, the main meal of the day is generally served in the middle of the day, sometime around 2 o'clock. A light snack is usually eaten in the late afternoon or early evening. Another snack, often just a dessert, is usually served later in the evening.

POLLO ASADO
BARBECUED CHICKEN

With all the barbecue sauces now available it may seem like too much trouble to make your own. Not so! This beats any the store has to offer.

INGREDIENTS:

1 can tomato purée
1/4 cup canned pineapple juice
2 tablespoons vegetable oil
1 tablespoon fresh parsley, chopped
1 tablespoon sugar

1 teaspoon salt
1/2 teaspoon chili powder
1/8 teaspoon hot pepper sauce
1/4 teaspoon pepper
1 3-pound broiler-fryer cut in pieces, or 6 chicken breasts

Prepare grill. Mix tomato purée, pineapple juice, oil, salt, parsley, sugar, hot pepper sauce, chili powder and pepper. Cut chicken into serving pieces. Brush each piece of chicken with tomato-pineapple sauce and place chicken over hot coals on grill. Cook for 45 minutes to 1 hour, brushing on sauce and and turning often. Serve with a rice dish and pineapple slices.

❖————————————❖————————————❖

CORDERO EN VINO TINTO
RED WINE LAMB

Yes, this takes time to prepare but when it's done and you're ready to dig into this delicious meal, you won't mind the effort.

INGREDIENTS:

4 pounds lamb shanks
3 dried California chiles
3 dried pasilla negro chiles
1 cup red wine
1/4 teaspoon ginger
1/2 teaspoon garlic powder

1 teaspoon cumin
1 teaspoon oregano
1/2 teaspoon salt
1/2 teaspoon pepper
1/8 teaspoon chili powder
Water

In a large saucepan, cover California and pasilla negro chiles with water. Bring to a boil and let stand until softened, about 45 minutes. Drain and clean discarding stems and seeds. In a blender, purée softened chiles, wine, ginger, garlic, cumin, oregano, chili powder and salt and pepper. Press mixture through a sieve to remove bits of peel. Place lamb shanks in a baking dish and coat with chile mixture. Cover and let sit in refrigerator for 5 hours, or overnight. Remove from refrigerator and bring to room temperature before cooking. Preheat oven to 350°F. Cover dish with foil and bake for 2 hours, or until tender. Turn meat in marinade every hour, making sure to recover with foil. Let cool. Serve on the bone with a five bean salad, or remove the meat from the bones, discarding bones, and serving with greens and chiles. Serves 6.

CARNE CON CHILE VERDE
GREEN CHILE MEAT LOAF

This recipe proves that meat loaf does not have to be the same as the one your mother used to make. It puts a new zing into an old favorite.

INGREDIENTS:

1 1/2 pounds lean ground beef
1 cup canned tomatoes, undrained
1 4-oz can green chiles, cleaned
seeded and chopped

1 cup soft bread crumbs
3 tablespoons dried onion flakes
1 1/2 teaspoon salt
1/4 teaspoon garlic salt

Preheat oven to 375° F. Combine ground beef, tomatoes, chiles, bread crumbs, onion flakes, garlic salt and salt. Mix well, using your hands. Place mixture in a large loaf pan and press lightly. Bake for 1 hour. Cover with enchilada sauce if desired. Serves 6.

❖————————————❖————————————❖

PICADILLO
MEXICAN HASH

This recipe is so versatile you can throw in almost anything. It makes a great meal and cleans up leftovers.

INGREDIENTS:

1 pound ground pork
1 pound ground beef
1 large onion, chopped
1/4 teaspoon garlic powder
2 medium tomatoes, peeled,
seeded and chopped
1 Granny Smith apple, peeled
and grated
1 tablespoon sugar
1/4 cup beef broth
4 tablespoons almond slivers

3 tablespoons black olives, pitted
and chopped
2 tablespoons chili powder
1/4 teaspoon cinnamon
1/4 teaspoon cumin
1 tablespoon vinegar
1/4 cup raisins, softened in
warm water
1/2 teaspoon oregano
Salt
Pepper

In a large skillet, cook pork, beef and onion until meat begins to brown. Add the tomatoes and beef broth and mix well. Simmer for 15 minutes before adding garlic powder, tomatoes, sugar, almonds, black olives, chili powder, cinnamon, cumin, vinegar, oregano and raisins. Bring to a boil. Add apples and simmer over medium low heat for 1/2 hour, stirring often. Serve with a side of refried beans and corn bread. Serves 8.

Barbeque Chicken with Five Bean Salad

POLLO CON SALSA D'UOVO
CHICKEN IN EGG AND LEMON SAUCE

The lemon sauce gives this chicken dish a fresh and tasty flavor. Serve with a side of Cilantro Rice to complete the feast.

INGREDIENTS:

4 chicken breasts	1/2 teaspoon oregano
2 tablespoons olive oil	2 egg yolks
2 tablespoons butter	3 tablespoons fresh parsley,
3 tablespoons flour	chopped
2 cups chicken broth	1 teaspoon lemon juice
1 clove garlic	4 slices of lemon
1 bay leaf	Salt and pepper

Season chicken with salt and pepper. In a skillet, heat oil, butter and garlic and add chicken breasts. Fry until golden brown, approximately 10 minutes. Remove and set chicken aside. Drain off all but 2 tablespoons of leftover oil. Add the flour to the oil and stir for 1 minute. Add broth and bring to a boil, stirring continuously. Return chicken to the pan. Add the bay leaf and oregano and cover. Simmer for 30 minutes, until tender. Remove chicken breasts from pan and place in a warm serving dish. Remove herbs from sauce and discard. Combine the egg yolks and lemon juice with 3 tablespoons of the sauce and add to the pan, stirring continuously until mixture thickens. Do not bring to a boil. Salt and pepper to taste. Pour sauce over chicken and garnish with lemon slices and fresh parsley. Serves 4.

❖ ─────────────────── ❖ ─────────────────── ❖

POLLO EN CHIPOTLE
CHICKEN IN CHIPOTLE CHILE SAUCE

I've loved this recipe ever since the first time it was served to me by my friend, Maria. I've adapted her original recipe to suit my own taste.

INGREDIENTS:

1 4-pound chicken, cut into pieces	1/2 medium onion, sliced thin
1 tablespoon chicken bouillon	1 16-ounce can stewed tomatoes
granules	1 1/2 teaspoons cumin
1/2 cup green chiles, diced	1/2 teaspoon cloves
5 canned chipotle chiles	3 cups water
1/2 teaspoon garlic powder	2 bay leaves
1 teaspoon oregano	Salt and pepper

Combine chiles, undrained tomatoes, chipotle chiles, garlic, oregano, cumin, clove and pepper in a blender and purée. Stir in bouillon granules. Set aside. In a large pot, place chicken, water, bay leaves and salt. Bring to a boil. Cover and simmer on low heat for 45 minutes. Drain broth. Add chipotle chile sauce and onion to chicken. Stir to coat chicken with sauce. Bring to a boil. Simmer on low heat for 20 minutes. Serves 4.

CHULETA DE CORDERO EN PIMIENTO
RED PEPPER LAMB CHOPS

This is an excellent choice for entertaining because it's so easy to prepare. You will delight your guests with the taste as well as the presentation.

INGREDIENTS:

12 1/2 inch thick lamb rib chops, trimmed
4 red bell peppers

2 tablespoons olive oil
Salt and pepper
Paprika

Prepare chiles as directed on page 17. Reserve juices and discard seeds. Cut peppers into strips. Place peppers in a pan and cover with reserved juice. Add 1 tablespoon olive oil. Set aside. Preheat broiler. Rub lamb with salt and pepper and paprika. Brush with 1 teaspoon oil. Broil to desired doneness, about 6 minutes for medium. Pour pepper mixture over lamb chops. Serve with ranch corn or other vegetable dish. Serves 6.

❖━━━━━━━━━❖━━━━━━━━━❖

SALSA DE POLLO CON CHAMPIÑONES
CHICKEN AND MUSHROOM SAUCE

Here is another wonderful selection for a dinner party. Its first class taste will ensure your success as an entertainer.

INGREDIENTS:

2 frying chickens, cut in serving pieces
1 16-oz can tomatoes, undrained
1 lb fresh mushrooms, cleaned and sliced
2 canned green chiles, seeded

1/4 cup oil
1/2 cup onion, chopped
1/4 teaspoon garlic powder
1 cup chicken broth
1 cup sour cream
1 1/2 teaspoons salt

Brown chicken in hot oil in a large pan. Transfer to a large pot. Sauté mushrooms in remaining oil in skillet. Spoon over chicken. Set pan with oil to one side. Combine tomatoes, chilies, onion, and garlic in a blender and purée. Pour purée into remaining oil in skillet, bring to a boil. Cook for 5 minutes, stirring in chicken stock and salt. Pour sauce over chicken and mushrooms in large pan. Cover and simmer on low for 1 hour, until chicken is tender. Just before serving, add sour cream and stir until heated through. Serve with rice. Serves 8.

❖━━━━━━━━━❖━━━━━━━━━❖

A WORD ABOUT SALSA:

Coat beef or chicken with salsa before grilling or baking for more flavor. Or, serve fresh, chunky salsa on the side to accommodate individual tastes. Not only does this add flavor, but adds color to the overall presentation.

CHILE RELLENOS
FILLED CHILES

There are many ways to stuff chiles, below are two different types of Chile Rellenos, the standard cheese filling and a flavorful combination of beef, pork, almonds, and raisins. Use your imagination, or any of the tasty filling recipes on pages 42 through 45.

INGREDIENTS:

2 medium onion, chopped	4 tablespoons raisins
2 medium tomatoes, chopped	8 whole canned chiles, seeded
1/8 teaspoon garlic powder	4 eggs
2 tablespoon oil	1/2 cup flour
1/2 pound ground beef	Oil for frying
1/2 pound ground pork	1 teaspoon salt
4 tablespoons sliced almonds	1/2 teaspoon pepper

Sauté onions in oil until tender. Add garlic powder and ground meats and cook until brown, scrambling meat while cooking. Add tomatoes, salt, pepper, almonds and raisins. Cook on low. In a separate pan, beat egg whites until stiff and add beaten egg yolks. Stuff chiles with meat filling. Roll stuffed chiles in flour and dip in egg batter. Heat 2 inches of oil in a deep skillet and fry chiles until lightly browned, turning often. Place on paper towels to absorb excess oils before serving. Serves 8.

❖━━━━━━━━━━━━❖━━━━━━━━━━━━❖

CHILE RELLENO CON QUESO
CHEESE FILLED CHILES

This is the most common version of Chile Relleno.

INGREDIENTS:

1/4 pound Monterey Jack cheese	2 eggs, separated
1 7 ounce can whole green chiles, seeded and kept whole	Flour
	Salt and pepper

Cut cheese in 1/2 inch thick rectangles, 1 inch long. Wrap cheese in chile and roll in flour that has been salt and peppered to taste. For the batter; beat egg whites until stiff and beat yolks lightly. Add yolks into whites and fold in 2 tablespoons of flour. Gently drop the floured chiles into the batter, one at a time. Place battered chiles on a plate and slide into a pan of moderately hot oil. Fry until golden brown, turning and basting to ensure even cooking. Place on paper towels to drain excess oil. Serves 4.

❖━━━━━━━━━━━━❖━━━━━━━━━━━━❖

A WORD ABOUT CHILI POWDER:
One long dried red chile is the equivalent of one tablespoon chili powder.

Fajitas and warm tortillas with Guacamole and salsa.

ASADO DE RES MEXICANO
MARINATED BEEF ROAST

With just a little preparation time and overnight marinating, you can make a plain roast taste like nothing you've ever had before.

INGREDIENTS:

1 clove garlic, minced	2 tablespoons water
1 4-pound beef roast, rolled	2 tablespoons flour
1 3/4 cups dry red wine	1 bay leaf
1 tablespoon lime juice	Salt
3 tablespoons olive oil	Pepper

Mix garlic, bay leaf, wine, lime juice, salt and pepper in a large casserole dish. Place the roast in the casserole dish and coat with mixture. Cover dish and marinate in refrigerator overnight, turning occasionally. Remove roast from dish and pat dry. Preheat oven to 375° F Heat oil in a skillet and brown roast on all sides. Salt and pepper to taste and place in a Dutch Oven. Pour marinade over roast and cover. Cook for 2 hours. Uncover and bake for another 15 to 30 minutes. Remove meat and place on a warm platter. Use drippings for gravy and serve with rice and beans. Serves 6.

❖————————————————❖————————————————❖

PUERCO EN MOLE VERDE
GREEN MOLE AND PORK

INGREDIENTS:

1 1/2 pound pork loin roast	1/4 cup hulled squash seeds
3 cups water	1 13-ounce can tomatillos
5 romaine lettuce leaves	2 cloves garlic minced
1/4 cup parsley	1 canned whole green chile
2 tablespoons cilantro	1 tablespoon oil
1 small onion, chopped	1/4 teaspoon cumin

Trim fat from pork and cut pork loin into 1 inch pieces. In a large saucepan place roast chunks, water, 1/2 onion, 1 clove garlic, salt and pepper to taste. Bring to a boil, skimming foam from surface. Cover and simmer on low for 1 hour. Toast squash seeds in a small skillet until lightly browned, stirring often. Grind cooled squash seeds in a blender and set aside. Drain canned tomatillos and combine with chile, lettuce, remaining onion, garlic, parsley and cilantro in a blender. Blend until fine. Drain meat, reserving broth. Return meat to pan. Heat oil in a skillet and sauté squash seeds for 2 minutes. Add ground tomatillo mixture and cook over low heat for 5 minutes. Add 1 cup strained reserved broth and stir. Pour mixture over meat. Add 1/2 teaspoon salt and cumin and simmer on low for 20 to 30 minutes. Add more broth to taste. Serves 4.

CARNE A LA MEXICANA
MEXICAN MEAT LOAF

Here we have another simple but fulfilling meal that I have found to be very popular with the men I know, especially the young ones.

INGREDIENTS:

1 pound ground beef
1/2 pound ground pork
1/2 cup onion, chopped
2/3 cup uncooked oats
1 egg, beaten
1 cup enchilada sauce

2 hard-boiled eggs, cut in half lengthwise
1/4 cup pimento-stuffed green olives, sliced
1 teaspoon salt
1/4 teaspoon pepper

Preheat oven to 350°F. Combine ground beef, ground pork, onion, oats, beaten egg, salt, pepper, and 1/2 cup enchilada sauce, mixing well. Pack half of the meat mixture into an average size loaf pan. Arrange hard boiled eggs in a row down center of loaf. Arrange olive slices on either side of eggs, gently press eggs and olives into meat. Cover with remaining half of meat mixture. Top with remaining 1/2 cup sauce. Bake for 1 hour.

❖———————————————————❖———————————————————❖

CASEROLA DE POLLO Y ARROZ
CHICKEN AND RICE CASSEROLE

Words cannot describe the flavor of this wonderful dish. And it tastes even better as a leftover.

INGREDIENTS:

2 whole chicken breasts
1/4 medium onion, chopped
1/8 teaspoon garlic powder
1 8 1/2 oz canned peas, drained
15 large Spanish green olive
1/2 teaspoon oregano
1 teaspoon salt
1/2 teaspoon pepper

1 tablespoon butter
1 cup uncooked long grain rice, rinsed, drained
1 cup canned tomatoes, undrained
6 peppercorns
1 quart water
Salt

Put chicken breasts in large pot. Add water, garlic powder, onion, pepper-corns and salt to taste. Bring to a boil. Cover and simmer on low heat for 45 minutes, or until tender. Drain chicken and reserve broth. Shred meat with fingers or by using 2 forks. Add olives, peas, oregano, 1 teaspoon salt and pepper, let sit. Preheat oven to 350°F. Heat butter in a large skillet. Add rice and sauté until lightly browned. Pour tomatoes over rice and press with a spoon. Let simmer for 5 minutes. Pour into a 3 quart casserole dish and add chicken mixture. Lightly mix. Strain 2 1/2 cups broth into mixture adding more if needed to cover mixture. Bake covered for 1 hour. Let stand covered for 15 minutes before serving. Serves 6.

PESCADO Y MARISCO
SEAFOOD

S eafood plays a significant roll in Mexican cooking. Mexico's west coast simply abounds with seafood making it possible to have fresh fish tacos, or lobster salad, at most restaurants at any time of the year. With typical Mexican flair, seafood is very often flavored with salsas or marinated with lime or lemon juice.

❖————————————————❖————————————————❖

CEVICHE
MARINATED FISH

Ceviche is most often served as an appetizer, however, many people like to serve Civiche at lunch along with a light salad.

INGREDIENTS:

1 pound white fish fillets, cut in bite sized pieces
1 large tomato, diced

1/3 cup onion, chopped fine
1/2 cup lime juice
Salt

Rinse fish and dry with paper towels before cutting into small pieces. Pour lime juice into a bowl and add fish. Stir gently and refrigerate, covered, overnight. Fish will be opaque when done. Drain fish and rinse lightly, but not enough to rinse out the lime. Drain and return to bowl. Add tomato, onion and salt to taste. Refrigerate for 30 minutes to blend flavors. Serve with tortilla chips. Makes 6 servings.

❖————————————————❖————————————————❖

BACALAO FESTIVO
HOLIDAY CODFISH

INGREDIENTS:

1 pound salted codfish (1 piece)
5 pickled chiles, seeded and cut in strips
2 small onions, peeled
3 medium tomatoes, peeled,

seeded and chopped
3 canned pimentos, cut in strips
1/2 cup pimento-stuffed olives
1 tablespoons chopped parsley
2 cloves garlic, peeled

Soak codfish for 3 hours in cold water, changing water often. Drain and put in saucepan, covering with water. Add 1 onion, and simmer, covered, until fish flakes easily when tested with fork. Drain. Salt and pepper to taste. Puree tomatoes, 1 onion and garlic in a blender. Add oil to sauce and cook in a skillet, stirring often. Mix in chile and pimento strips. Place codfish on a plate and cover with sauce. Garnish with olives and parsley.

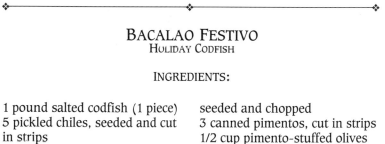

Ceviche and shrimp dip.

CAMARONES RICOS
RICH SHRIMP

Rich is the only word I can find to describe this wonderful creation.

INGREDIENTS:

1 lb shrimp, peeled and deveined	1 tablespoon parsley, minced
1 5 ounce can evaporated milk	1/2 teaspoon Worcestershire
2 tablespoons butter	sauce
1 slice bacon, chopped	1/2 cup white wine
2 ounces Swiss cheese, shredded	Salt and white pepper
2 tablespoons dairy sour cream	Steamed white rice

Mix butter and bacon in a large non-stick pan. Over medium heat, cook until bacon is lightly browned. Add shrimp and cook until pink, stirring for about 2 minutes. Place cooked shrimp on a warm plate, leaving juices in pan. Add wine to pan and cook until mixture is reduced to 1/3 cup. Add milk and simmer for 1 minute, stirring constantly. Add Worcestershire sauce, salt and pepper to taste. Add cheese gradually, stirring until melted. Return shrimp to pan. Cook on low for 2 minutes, stirring constantly. Stir in sour cream and blend well. Do not boil. Serve over steamed white rice and garnish with parsley. Serves 4.

❖————————————————❖————————————————❖

HUACHINANGO AL HORNO
BAKED RED SNAPPER

Even if fish is not your favorite food, you will not be able to resist this dish. Serve with a simple rice dish to complete the meal.

INGREDIENTS:

2 pounds red snapper fillets	1/4 cup white wine
1 medium onion, sliced	1/2 cup black olives, pitted
2 tablespoons olive oil	1 teaspoon cumin
5 medium tomatoes, chopped	Juice from 1 lemon
1/8 teaspoon garlic powder	1 cup milk
1 teaspoon oregano	Salt
2 tablespoons capers	Pepper

Cut fish into 8 pieces and place in a casserole dish. Mix oregano in milk and pour over fish. Refrigerate for 2 hours, covered. In a large skillet, sauté onion in oil. Add tomatoes, garlic powder, capers, wine, cumin, lemon juice and olives. Simmer for 15 minutes or until thickened. Drain fish and dry with paper towels. Make 8 sturdy aluminum foil squares, 12 inches wide. Place a fish fillet on each foil square. Spoon equal amounts of vegetable mixture over each piece of fish. Fold foil until securely sealed. Put foil packs on a baking sheet and cook at 350° F for 30 minutes. Fish is done when it flakes easily with a fork. Garnish with cilantro. Serves 8.

CAMARON A LA VERACRUZANA
VERACRUZ SHRIMP

This is yet another excellent recipe for my favorite shellfish, Veracruz style.

INGREDIENTS:

1 pound fresh medium shrimp, peeled, and deveined
12 pimento stuffed green olives
5 small tomatoes, chopped and peeled
1 large green pepper
1 small onion, chopped

1 1/2 teaspoons capers
1/2 teaspoon sugar
1/2 teaspoon salt
1/2 teaspoon pepper
2 tablespoons oil
1 tablespoon oil
Lemon juice

Cut green pepper into 1x1 inch pieces. Sauté onion and green pepper . Add tomatoes, capers, olives, sugar and salt. Bring mixture to a boil. Cover and simmer on medium low heat for 20 minutes. Taste sauce and add salt to taste. In a large skillet, heat 2 tablespoons of oil and add shrimp. Cook over medium heat until pink, approximately 2 minutes. Sprinkle lemon juice over shrimp and add sauce. Let simmer over low heat for 3 to 4 more minutes. Serve hot. Serves 4.

❖————————————————❖————————————————❖

PESCADO FRITO
MEXICAN FRIED FISH

Once again, you can take what is usually an ordinary dish and turn it into something really special. Wait until you try this!

INGREDIENTS:

1 pound fish fillets, fresh or frozen
2 tablespoons lime juice
1/2 cup flour

1/4 cup oil
Salt and pepper

INGREDIENTS FOR SAUCE:

2 tablespoons olive oil
1 small onion, chopped
1/2 cup green pepper, chopped
1/2 cup celery, chopped
1/2 teaspoon garlic powder

2 tablespoons dry sherry
1 cup canned peeled tomatoes, drained and chopped
Salt and pepper
Saffron

Sprinkle fish with lime juice, salt and pepper and let sit. Heat olive oil and add green pepper, celery, onion, and garlic. Sauté until tender. Add sherry, tomatoes and salt and pepper to taste. Add dash of saffron. Simmer, stirring occasionally. Drain fish and coat with flour. Heat oil and fry fish until lightly brown, turning once. Drain fish and place on paper towel to absorb excess oils. Serve on warm plates, topping with sauce. Serves 4.

77

PESCADO A LA NARANJA
ORANGE FISH

Here is a sinfully delicious creation that is really very good for you. I like to garnish this recipe with thin orange slices.

INGREDIENTS:

4 fish fillets	1 large tomato, peeled, seeded
1/4 cup lime juice	and diced
4 tablespoons olive oil	1/2 cup orange juice
3 scallions, chopped fine	2 tablespoons capers, drained
1/8 teaspoon garlic powder	2 tablespoons dry sherry

Place fish fillets in a baking dish and sprinkle with salt, pepper and lime juice. Let stand for 1/2 hour. Preheat oven to 350°F. Using a tablespoon of olive oil, lightly grease a shallow baking dish. Place fish, salt and pepper side down in baking dish. In a small bowl, mix scallions, tomato, garlic, remaining olive oil, and capers. Spread mixture over fish. Bake for 10 minutes before pouring orange juice and sherry over fish. Bake for another 10 minutes, until fish is done. Serves 4.

❖————————————————❖————————————————❖

PESCADO CAMPECHANO
FISH CAMPECHE STYLE

Try this incredible dish on someone who doesn't like fish. You will create a fan for life. Serve with black beans (recipe page 82).

INGREDIENTS:

1 pound fish fillets, fresh or	1 cup water
frozen	1/4 cup onion, chopped
1 cup orange juice	1 teaspoon chili powder
1 6 ounce can tomato paste	Salt and pepper

Place fish in a medium pan and add water to cover. Add 1/2 cup of orange juice. Bring to a boil. Simmer on low for 10 minutes, or until fish flakes when tested with a fork. Drain and skim, if necessary. Cut fish into finger-sized pieces. Return to pan. In a separate saucepan, combine remaining orange juice, tomato paste, 1 cup of water, onion, and chili powder. Bring to a boil. Season with salt and pepper to taste. Pour sauce over fish and simmer until sauce thickens. Serves 6.

❖————————————————❖————————————————❖

A WORD ABOUT SUBSTITUTIONS:

Substitute your favorite fish or seafood when preparing recipes in this section.

PESCADO BLANCO CON SALSA DE AGUACATE
WHITE FISH WITH AVOCADO SAUCE

Avocados give this white fish a creamy, savory flavor that everyone at your table will relish.

INGREDIENTS:

1 1/2 pounds white fish fillets, fresh or frozen	1 bay leaf, crushed
5 peppercorns	3 or 4 onion slices
1/4 teaspoon salt	Juice of 1/2 lemon
	Water

INGREDIENTS FOR AVOCADO SAUCE:

1 large ripe avocado, peeled and sliced	1 teaspoon lemon juice
1/2 teaspoon Worcestershire sauce	1/2 cup milk
	4 parsley sprigs
1/2 cup whipping cream	1/2 teaspoon white pepper
	1/2 teaspoon salt

To prepare avocado sauce: place avocado slices, whipping cream, milk, lemon juice, salt, pepper, Worcestershire sauce and parsley in blender and blend until smooth. Cook over medium heat in a saucepan, stirring often, do not bring to a boil. Set aside. Keep warm. To prepare fish: place fish in large skillet and add water to cover. Add peppercorns, bay leaf, salt, onion slices and lemon juice. Bring to a boil. Cover and simmer on low heat for 10 minutes or until fish flakes easily when tested. Drain fish and place on a warm plate. Pour sauce over fish and garnish with parsley. Serve hot.

❖ ──────────── ❖ ──────────── ❖

TACOS DE PESCADO BLANCO
WHITE FISH TACOS

Fish tacos seem to be a gaining popularity at many Mexican restaurants. Try this recipe to make tasty, as well as healthy Fish Tacos at home.

INGREDIENTS:

1 pound white fish fillets	1 cup hot cooked spinach, chopped
1 medium tomato, chopped fine	
1/4 cup scallions, chopped fine	8 taco shells
2 tablespoons canned green chiles	1 cup sour cream
2 tablespoons lemon juice	Salt and pepper

Poach fish with lemon juice and water to cover until fish is opaque and flakes easily with a fork. Combine tomatoes, scallions, salt and chiles in a bowl. Drain fish and cut into small chunks, removing any bones or skin. Place equal amounts of fish on each taco shell, add hot spinach and top with tomato sauce. Garnish with sour cream and serve. Serves 8.

FRIJOLES Y ARROZ
RICE AND BEANS

B eans and rice are truly the staples of the Mexican diet. Almost every meal includes a portion of one or both. Beans are especially important since they are served even at breakfast and because of their nutritional value. Many varieties of beans are used in Mexican cooking, with black, pinto, navy and kidney beans most often used in meal preparation. Spices play a key role in the preparation of bean and rice dishes and of course, the inclusion of chiles makes each dish a delectable delight.

❖───────────────❖───────────────❖

FRIJOLES
BEANS

The most commonly eaten food in the Mexican diet, beans can be used as a filler or a side dish. This is an easy way to prepare one of my favorite foods.

INGREDIENTS:

1 pound red beans
1 1/2 quarts water

1/2 cup lard or bacon drippings
Salt

Soak beans overnight. Add more water to cover and add salt. Cook on very low heat until very tender. Using a potato masher, mash the beans before adding very hot bacon drippings or lard. Continue cooking until the fat has been absorbed, stirring often to avoid sticking. Serves 6.

❖───────────────❖───────────────❖

PREPARATION OF REFRIED BEANS

Heat additional fat in a frying pan and add beans (prepared as above). Cook and stir until beans become dry. Serves 6.

❖───────────────❖───────────────❖

FRIJOLES A LA OLLA
BOILED BEANS FROM THE POT

Cook beans as shown in the basic recipe above, but do not mash or add bacon drippings or lard. When beans have been cooked until tender, ladle into soup bowls. Garnish with chopped onion, shredded Cheddar cheese and cooked, chopped chiles to taste and serve on the side.

All beans freeze beautifully, so prepare ahead and keep a healthy amount handy in the freezer for quick meals.

Stuffed Bell Peppers and Spanish Rice.

FRIJOLES NEGROS
BLACK BEANS

This is so tasty! I like to garnish with a pile of shredded cheese and eat them with tortilla chips. They also keep well in the refrigerator for days.

INGREDIENTS:

1 cup dried black beans	1/4 teaspoon garlic powder
1 medium onion, cut in half with one half chopped	3 tablespoons lard
	1 teaspoon salt

Place beans in a large saucepan and cover with hot water. Boil for 2 minutes then remove and let stand for 1 hour. Drain and rinse. Add more hot water to cover beans and bring to a boil. Reduce heat and add onion half and 2 tablespoons lard. Simmer, covered, for 2 hours. Add salt. Cover and simmer for 2 more hours or until beans are tender. Add more hot water if needed to keep beans covered. Sauté chopped onion in remaining lard until brown. Remove and discard onion half from saucepan. Add beans, including cooking liquid, to skillet. Mash some, but not all, of the beans. Cook until thickened but not dry. Serves 4.

❖————————————————❖————————————————❖

FRIJOLES CON PUERCO
BEANS AND PORK

Good old pork and beans. These is not the same as Mom used to give you, but are very popular with kids everywhere.

INGREDIENTS:

1 1/2 cups dried black beans	1 pound boneless pork
1 small onion, chopped	2 tablespoons lard
2 cloves garlic, minced	Salt

INGREDIENTS FOR GARNISH:

Hot salsa (see recipe page 19)	2 medium tomatoes, chopped
5 green onions, chopped	2 jalapeño chiles, sliced
6 radishes, diced	1/2 cup cilantro, chopped

Cover beans with very hot water and boil for 2 minutes. Remove and let stand for 1 hour. Drain and rinse. Add fresh hot water to cover beans and bring to a boil. Add onion and garlic and simmer for 2 hours. Cut pork into chunks and salt to taste. Heat the lard in a skillet and add seasoned pork. Brown pork and drain. Add pork to beans with 1 1/2 teaspoons salt. Cover and simmer for 2 to 3 1/2 hours, or until beans are tender. Add hot water to keep beans covered. When ready to serve, garnish with cilantro and place chopped green onions, radishes, tomatoes, and jalapeño chiles on a side dish and serve on the side along with hot salsa. Serves 6.

ARROZ A LA ESPAÑOLA
SPANISH RICE

Using chicken or beef broth, instead of water, deepens the flavor of this very traditional Mexican side dish.

INGREDIENTS:

1 cup white rice, rinsed
4 cups chicken or beef broth,
or water
1 small onion, diced
2 tablespoons oil

1/2 cup canned mixed vegetables,
cooked
1/2 cup tomato sauce
1 teaspoon salt
1 teaspoon pepper

Sauté onion in oil and add the rice. Stir constantly over a low heat until the rice starts to brown. Add tomato sauce, salt and pepper and liquid. Bring to a boil. Cover pot tightly and reduce heat, cooking for 15 minutes without removing the cover. Add the vegetables and cook until the rice is tender. Serves 4.

❖―――――――❖―――――――❖

PICADILLO DE ARROZ
SEASONED RICE

Rice is seldom served plain in Mexican cooking. A few spices and vegetables are added and an exciting side dish is created.

INGREDIENTS:

1 1/2 cup instant rice
1/2 medium onion
2 small tomatoes, peeled
1/8 teaspoon ground cloves
1/8 teaspoon cinnamon
2 tablespoons butter

1 tablespoon oil
1 1/2 cups pork broth
1/3 cup frozen peas, thawed
1/2 cup potato, diced and peeled
1 teaspoon salt
1 teaspoon pepper

Purée tomatoes, onion, cloves and cinnamon in a blender or food processor. Heat butter and oil in a large pot and add rice. Cook over medium heat until lightly browned, stirring occasionally. Add tomato mixture. Cook for 3 minutes, stirring constantly. Add broth, salt and pepper and simmer, covered, until most of the liquid is gone. Add peas and potato and stir. Steam over low heat for 30 to 45 minutes, until rice is tender. Serves 6.

❖―――――――❖―――――――❖

A WORD ABOUT CILANTRO

Cilantro is an often used spice in Mexican cooking. Best when used fresh, it looses much of its flavor when dried. Cilantro has a pleasant, cool flavor and goes well with onions, chiles and tomatoes when used in salsas.

ARROZ Y CHILE
RICE AND CHILES

Here we combine two of the most important and beloved foods in the Mexican diet. Serve with a side of beans and warm tortillas.

INGREDIENTS:

1 1/2 cup instant rice
2 canned green chiles, sliced
1/8 teaspoon garlic powder
3 tablespoons oil
1 small onion, chopped fine

1 1/2 cups chicken broth
1/2 cup Monterey Jack cheese, shredded
1/2 teaspoon salt
1/2 teaspoon pepper

Heat oil in a large pot and add rice, cooking until lightly browned. Add onion and garlic powder and cook until onion is tender. Add chile strips and broth. Simmer, covered, until most of the broth is absorbed. Steam on a low temperature for 15 to 30 minutes, until rice is tender. Add salt and pepper to taste. Before serving, add shredded cheese to rice and mix well. Cover and steam gently to melt cheese. Serves 4.

❖─────────────❖─────────────❖

ARROZ VERDE
GREEN RICE

With very little time and effort, a bright and savory side dish is created. Serve with a side of black beans for a contrasting effect.

INGREDIENTS:

1/2 cups instant rice
1/2 cups chicken broth
1 large green pepper, cleaned and seeded
1/2 medium onion

2 cloves garlic
1/4 cup fresh parsley
3 tablespoons oil
Salt
Pepper

Finely chop green pepper, onion, garlic and parsley in a blender or food processor. In a small pan, heat 1 tablespoon oil and add green pepper mixture. Cook for 3 minutes, stirring. Heat 2 tablespoons oil in a large pot and add rice. Cook over medium heat until lightly browned, stirring often. Stir in green pepper mixture, broth and salt. Simmer, covered, until most of the liquid is absorbed. Reduce heat to low and steam for 15 to 30 minutes. Rice is done when tender. Salt and pepper to taste. Serves 6.

❖─────────────❖─────────────❖

ARROZ Y CHORIZO
CHORIZO AND RICE

INGREDIENTS:

1 1/2 cup instant rice
1 1/2 cups chicken broth
1/4 pound chorizo (see page 90)
1/3 cup onion, chopped
1/4 cup frozen peas

1 medium tomato, peeled and
chopped
Avocado slices
Salt
Pepper

Remove casing from chorizo and discard. Scramble chorizo and cook over medium heat until browned. Remove chorizo from pan and set aside. Using the same pan, cook rice over medium heat for 4 minutes. Add onion and cook until onion is tender. Add tomato and cook until tomato is soft enough to mash into rice. Return chorizo to the pan and add peas and chicken broth. Let simmer until most of the liquid is gone. Steam on very low heat for 15 to 20 minutes, until rice is tender. Add salt and pepper to taste. Garnish with avocado slices. Serves 4.

❖——————————————❖——————————————❖

ARROZ CON CILANTRO
RICE WITH CILANTRO

INGREDIENTS:

1 1/2 cup instant rice
1 1/2 cups chicken broth
1/2 small onion, chopped fine
2 tablespoons oil
2 cloves garlic, pressed

1/8 teaspoon ground cumin
1/8 teaspoon oregano
1/2 cup lightly packed cilantro
sprigs
1 teaspoon salt

Heat oil in a skillet and add rice. Fry until rice begins to brown. Add onion, garlic and cumin. Cook onion until tender but not browned. Add broth, cilantro, oregano and salt. Cover and boil until rice absorbs most of the fluid. Steam on very low heat for 30 to 45 minutes, or until rice is tender.

❖——————————————❖——————————————❖

SOPA DE ARROZ
RED RICE

INGREDIENTS:

1 1/2 cups instant rice
1 1/2 cups chicken broth
1 clove garlic, pressed

3 tablespoons oil
1 8-ounce can tomato sauce
1/2 medium onion, chopped

Mix garlic with salt to make a paste. In a large pot, heat oil and add rice. Cook over medium heat until lightly browned. Add garlic paste and onion and cook until onion is tender. Stir in chicken broth and tomato sauce. Cover and simmer until much of the liquid is absorbed. Steam on very low heat for 30 to 45 minutes until rice is tender. Serves 6.

ARROZ CON CAMARON
RED RICE AND SHRIMP

When you are in a hurry but still want to make something special, this is the recipe to use. In this case, an hour can bring perfection.

INGREDIENTS:

1 pound shelled green shrimp	1/4 teaspoon marjoram
1/2 cup onion, chopped	1 cup uncooked rice
1 clove garlic, minced	2 1/2 cups water
1 green pepper, seeded and	1/4 cup oil
sliced	Salt
1 6 ounce can tomato paste	Pepper

Sauté onion and garlic in oil until tender, about 5 minutes. Add green pepper and uncooked shrimp and cook until shrimp turn pink. Add tomato paste, water, marjoran and salt and pepper to taste. Bring to a boil and add rice, mixing well. Simmer, covered, on low heat for 20 to 30 minutes, until all liquid is absorbed by rice. Serves 6.

❖————————————————❖————————————————❖

FRIJOLES PUERCOS
BEANS, PIG STYLE

I think this recipe is called Beans, Pig Style, because everyone who eats them always asks for more!

INGREDIENTS:

1/2 pound bacon, cut in pieces	2 cups Monterey Jack cheese,
4 cups cooked Mexican beans,	1 can sardines in tomato sauce
undrained	1 chorizo sausage

Using a different pan, fry chorizos, removing casing first. Fry bacon until crisp and add beans a few spoonfuls at a time, mashing each spoonful and adding some of the bean fluid. Cook until mixture becomes thick and then add cheese, cut into cubes, and chorizo. Stir in sardines and cook until warmed thoroughly. Serve with tortilla chips.

❖————————————————❖————————————————❖

LENTEJAS CON FRUTA
LENTILS WITH FRUIT

Pineapple seems to make any recipe tastier and certainly more interesting. The bananas also add and unusual flavor.

INGREDIENTS:

3 pieces of bacon, cut in pieces
1 medium onion, chopped
1 pound lentils
2 quarts water

1/2 cup tomato sauce
Salt and pepper
Sliced bananas
Sliced pineapple

Fry bacon and onion, and add lentils, water and tomato sauce and salt and pepper to taste. Simmer over medium heat until lentils are tender and liquid thickens, approximately 2 hours. Serve with sliced bananas and pineapple.

ARROZ BLANCO CON ALCACHOFAS
WHITE RICE WITH ARTICHOKES

This is the perfect accompaniment to all barbequed meats. It also makes a popular dish for pot luck dinners.

INGREDIENTS:

2 cups rice, uncooked
1/4 cup olive oil
1 large onion, diced
5 cups chicken broth
1 cup peas, fresh or frozen

12 artichoke hearts, cooked
2 cloves garlic
1 can pimientos, sliced
Salt
Pepper

Fry rice in oil until it turns light brown. Add onion and garlic and sauté until onions become tender. Place onion and garlic in a casserole dish and add boiling broth, artichokes, peas, pimientos and salt and pepper to taste. Bake at 350° F until all liquid as been absorbed by the rice, approximately 35 minutes. Serves 6.

ARROZ RAPIDA
QUICK MEXICAN RICE

INGREDIENTS:

1 medium onion
1/2 teaspoon garlic salt
1/2 teaspoon salt
1 tablespoon butter
1 8-ounce can stewed tomatoes

1/2 cup chicken broth
1/2 teaspoon chili powder
1/8 teaspoon cumin
1 cup instant rice
Salt and pepper

Cut the onion in half and finely chop 1 half. Slice the other half very thin. Heat butter in a saucepan and add chopped onion, salt, pepper and garlic salt. Cook, stirring, until onion is tender. Add stewed tomatoes, broth, cumin and chili powder. Mash tomatoes with the back of a spoon and bring mixture to a boil. Stir in rice and onion slices. Cover and cook on very low heat for 15 minutes or until liquid is absorbed. Serves 4.

DESAYUNO Y ALMUERZO
BREAKFAST

An early morning breakfast, called *desayuno*, commonly consists of a cup of coffee with milk and a tortilla or piece of bread. Later in the morning a larger meal, *almuerzo*, is served. This meal usually includes beans, tortillas, eggs and chiles and is also served with coffee. For our purposes we have prepared a list of recipes that would be appropriately served as breakfast or a brunch. Personally, I love to eat breakfast at any time of the day, especially egg dishes.

❖————————————❖————————————❖

HUEVOS RANCHEROS
RANCH STYLE EGGS

This is the quintessential Mexican egg dish. The reason it's so popular is because it tastes so good. Serve with warm tortillas.

INGREDIENTS:

4 eggs	1 or 2 green chiles, peeled,
1 tablespoon onion, minced	mashed and strained
2 tablespoons oil	1/2 teaspoon oregano
1/8 teaspoon garlic powder	1 teaspoon salt
1 8 ounce can tomato sauce	1 teaspoon pepper

In a large skillet, sauté onion in oil until tender and add garlic, oregano, green chili, tomato sauce and salt and pepper. Simmer for 5 minutes letting the flavors blend. Poach or fry eggs and cover with sauce. Serve with a side of beans, tortillas and coffee. Serves 2.

❖————————————❖————————————❖

HUEVOS REVUELTOS
MEXICAN SCRAMBLED EGGS

This takes the boring out of scrambled eggs and puts a zing where you least expect it. Serve, of course, with warm tortillas.

INGREDIENTS:

4 eggs	1 tablespoon parsley, diced
1 tablespoon green pepper, diced	1 small green onion, diced
1 medium tomato	Salt
2 teaspoons milk	Pepper

Peel and cut tomato into squares, removing seeds. Beat eggs and add milk, tomato, parsley, green pepper, onion and salt and pepper to taste. Scramble in butter and serve with warm tortillas. Serves 2.

Huevos Rancheros and Refried Beans.

CHORIZO
MEXICAN SAUSAGE

This spicy sausage is used in everything from stews to egg dishes. As well as being a versatile ingredient when cooking, it freezes well, too.

INGREDIENTS:

1/2 pound ground beef	1 tablespoon oregano
1/2 pound ground pork	1 tablespoon paprika
1/2 pound ground pork fat	1/2 teaspoon cumin
5 dried hot 2 inch chiles	1/2 teaspoon sugar
1 teaspoon cumin seed	1/8 teaspoon cloves, ground
Oil for frying	1 teaspoon salt
1/2 cup wine vinegar	1 teaspoon pepper
1/2 teaspoon garlic powder	Sausage casings

Brown chiles and cumin seed in oil, stirring constantly. Drain and cool. Crush chiles. Mix chiles with all other ingredients except sausage casing. Allow flavors to blend by refrigerating in covered bowl for 24 hours. Press chorizo in sausage casings and tie with string every 6 inches. Refrigerate sausages on a rack until dry, at least 1 day, but not longer than 3 days. Cook sausages in a skillet with 4 tablespoons of water. Cover and cook slowly for 10 minutes. Uncover and cook, turning to brown sausages evenly. Makes 6 long sausages.

❖————————————————————❖————————————————————❖

CAMARON CON HUEVOS RANCHEROS
SHRIMP STYLE RANCH EGGS

This is a sinfully decadent and delectable dish that I have found to be an especially popular brunch entrée.

INGREDIENTS:

24 small or medium shrimp, halved horizontally	5 tablespoons butter
	8 eggs, beaten
4 green chiles, roasted, peeled and seeded	8 green onions, sliced thin
	12 corn tortillas
6 tablespoons sour cream, room temperature	Salt
	Pepper

In a skillet, melt butter over medium high heat. Add shrimp, onions and chiles and sauté until shrimp turn pink, about 1 minute. Reduce heat to medium low and add eggs. Gently stir mixture until just set. Season with salt and pepper and stir in sour cream. Remove from heat. Using a sharp knife, cut a slit in the side of each tortilla, forming a pocket. Spoon in the shrimp and egg mixture, dividing evenly. Transfer to platter. Garnish with salsa and a dollop of sour cream. Serves 10.

TORTILLA DE HUEVOS CON PAPAS Y ACEITUNAS
POTATO OLIVE OMELET

Potatoes and olives make an interesting combination. This omelet is easy to prepare and the chiles offer their usual zing.

INGREDIENTS:

1 large potato	3/4 cup Cheddar cheese, shredded
6 eggs	1/4 cup sliced green olives
2 tablespoons olive oil	1/2 teaspoon oregano
1/2 small onion, chopped	Salt
1/4 small green pepper, diced	Pepper

Boil potato in water until tender when pierced with a fork. When the potato is cool, peel and dice. Saute onion and bell pepper in 1 tablespoon olive oil until tender. Mix in potato, olives and oregano and cook until heated through. Carefully mix in cheese. Salt and pepper to taste. Cover and set aside. Heat remaining olive oil over medium-high heat. In another bowl, scramble the eggs. Add eggs to skillet. Using a spatula, carefully lift edges to allow uncooked portion of eggs to flow under cooked portion. Cook eggs just until they set. Spoon filling over half of eggs. Using a spatula, fold unfilled portion of eggs over filling. Serves 2.

❖————————————————❖————————————————❖

HUEVOS CON PAPAS Y CHORIZO
HEARTY EGGS WITH POTATOES AND CHORIZO

Hearty is the correct name for this wonderful meal. It's my absolute favorite breakfast dish. Serve with warm tortillas and a good cup of coffee.

INGREDIENTS:

2 large potatoes, peeled	1/2 cup onion, chopped fine
1/2 pound chorizo (see recipe page 91)	4 eggs
	1 avocado, sliced

Dice potatoes. Remove casing from chorizo and cook, scrambled, until brown. Add diced potatoes and onion. Cover pot and cook over medium heat for 15 minutes or until potatoes are tender. Remove cover. Make indentations for 4 eggs in potato mixture. Break an egg and place into each indentation. Replace cover and cook for 3 to 5 minutes or until eggs are set. Garnish with avocado slices and serve. Serves 4.

❖————————————————❖————————————————❖

A WORD ABOUT MARJORAM
One half teaspoon oregano leaves equals the flavor of one teaspoon marjoram leaves.

ENCHILADAS DE HUEVOS ESPAÑOL Y CHAMPIÑONES
CHILE AND MUSHROOM OMELET

I was lucky enough to find this recipe at a quaint Bed and Breakfast in the old mining town of Bisbee, Arizona.

INGREDIENTS:

8 eggs
3 tablespoons canned green chiles, diced
1 1/2 tablespoon scallions, chopped fine
1 cup mushrooms, sliced thin

4 tablespoons butter
1/4 teaspoon Tabasco sauce
1/2 cup Monterey Jack cheese, shredded
1 tablespoon water
Salt and pepper

Lightly beat together eggs, diced chiles, scallion, Tabasco sauce and water. Sauté mushrooms in 2 tablespoons butter until lightly browned. Drain excess fluid and remove mushrooms. Melt the remaining 2 tablespoons butter in the pan and pour in eggs. Cook until the omelet starts to set, lifting the edges to allow liquid to run over the edges. When the omelet is set, but still moist in the middle, add mushrooms and cheese evenly over half, fold to enclose filling. Cook for 2 minutes and serve. Serves 4.

❖————————————❖————————————❖

TORTA DE HUEVO A LA ESPAÑOLA
SPANISH OMELET

A favorite of both Norte-Americanos and Mexicans, this omelet is a flavorful dish with a beautiful presentation.

INGREDIENTS:

8 eggs
1 small onion, chopped fine
1 green pepper, chopped fine
3 tablespoons oil

2 8-ounce cans tomato sauce
1/2 cup milk
Salt
Pepper

Sauté onion and green pepper in hot oil until onion becomes tender. Add tomato sauce, salt and pepper to taste and simmer over low heat for 20 minutes. Prepare four separate omelets using 2 eggs and 2 tablespoons milk each. Serve omelets and top with sauce. Serves 4.

❖————————————❖————————————❖

FRIJOLES Y HUEVOS
STONED EGGS

This combines two of my favorite foods, eggs and beans. I think adding beans to almost anything is a good idea.

INGREDIENTS:

8 eggs, beaten
4 teaspoons butter

16 tablespoons finely mashed
refried beans (recipe page 80)

To make one omelet at a time; heat 1 teaspoon butter in heavy skillet. Add enough eggs to make one omelet. Cook and stir until set. Add 2 tablespoons of beans and stir. Cook for 1 to 2 minutes. Serves 4.

❖————————————————❖————————————————❖

HUEVOS VALLEJO
VALLEJO EGGS

INGREDIENTS:

6 eggs
2 canned green chiles, cut in
strips
1/4 cup Monterey Jack cheese,
shredded

1 16-ounce can whole tomatoes,
undrained
1 tablespoon butter
1 small onion, sliced
Salt and pepper

Sauté onion slices in butter. Stir in chile strips and tomatoes. Cook for 4 minutes, cutting tomatoes with a fork. Add salt and pepper to taste. Break eggs one at a time into a saucer and slide all eggs at once into the hot tomato sauce. Cover and simmer for 2 minutes. When eggs are almost set, sprinkle shredded cheese over eggs. Cook for 3 minutes or until eggs are completely set. Spoon sauce over eggs as they cook. Serves 6.

❖————————————————❖————————————————❖

SOUFFLÉ DE ELOTE
CORN SOUFFLE

Even though this is most often eaten for breakfast, it makes a great side dish, too. Serve with pork loin at dinner.

INGREDIENTS:

1 17-ounce, can whole corn
3 eggs, separated
1/2 medium onion, chopped fine

3 tablespoons butter
1/2 cup chopped green chiles
1/2 teaspoon salt and pepper

Heat oven to 375°F. Prepare a 1 1/2 quart baking dish by greasing and lightly dusting with flour. Set aside. In a skillet, sauté onion in butter until onion becomes tender. Add drained corn, cooked onion and egg yolks in blender or food processor. Process until corn is fine. Pour into a medium bowl. Add chiles and salt, stir. In a small bowl beat egg whites until stiff. Fold gently into corn mixture. Mix thoroughly. Place batter into prepared baking dish and bake for 10 minutes. Reduce heat to 350°F and bake 20 to 25 minutes. Soufflé is done when top begins to brown lightly and an inserted toothpick comes out clean. Serves 6.

OTROS PLATILLOS
SIDE DISHES

Vegetables in Mexican cookingare as unique as the people themselves. Potatoes, hominy, zucchini, squash, spinach and even nopalas (cactus leaves) turn up in every day Mexican cooking. Include a few additions, such as pastas, and you have a vast selection of side dishes at your Mexican feast.

❖――――――――――――❖――――――――――――❖

ESPINACA CON CHÎCHAROS
SPINACH WITH CHICK PEAS

INGREDIENTS:

10 ounces fresh spinach leaves
2 15-ounce cans chick peas (gar-banzo beans), rinsed drained
1 teaspoon cumin seeds
1 small dried red chile, crushed
10 whole black peppercorns

1 tablespoon red wine vinegar
1/2 cup olive oil
1 2 inch slice bread, trimmed
4 large cloves garlic,
1 tablespoon paprika
1/2 cup water

Grind cumin, chile and peppercorns in a spice grinder. Set aside. Heat oil in a large pan over medium high heat. Add bread and 2 cloves garlic and brown bread on both sides. Transfer garlic and bread to food processor. Add cumin, chili and peppercorn to mixture and blend well. Do not rinse skillet. Place skillet over high heat. Add remaining garlic cloves and paprika. Stir for 1 minute. Add 1/2 cup water and wine vinegar to skillet and bring to boil, stirring often. Add the food processor contents, chick peas and spinach leaves to skillet. Cook on medium for 10 minutes, until spinach is tender and mixture starts to thicken. Discard garlic. Serves 4.

❖――――――――――――❖――――――――――――❖

CACEROLA DE POZOLE CON TOCINO
BACON AND HOMINY CASSEROLE

INGREDIENTS:

1/2 pound bacon, sliced
2 15-oz cans hominy, drained
1 green pepper, chopped
1 small onion, chopped

1 16-oz can tomatoes, undrained
1 tablespoon sugar
1 tablespoon paprika
1/2 cup water

Fry bacon in a skillet. Drain, reserving 2 tablespoons drippings in skillet. Add green pepper and onion. Cook until tender. Add tomatoes with liquid, sugar and salt. Simmer for 10 minutes. Place in a greased baking dish. Crumble bacon over the top and mix with hominy. Pour tomato mixture over top. Bake at 325°F for 45 minutes. Serves 8.

MAIZ RANCHERO
RANCH CORN

This makes an excellent side dish to any meal. Serve with Barbequed Chicken or Tomato and Pepper Pork Chops.

INGREDIENTS:

6 slices bacon, diced
2 tablespoons onion, chopped
1 4 1/2-oz can of mushrooms, drained

2 12-oz cans whole-kernel corn with peppers, drained
3/4 cup Monterey Jack cheese, shredded

Fry bacon until cooked but not brown. Drain excess fat and add mushrooms and onion and sauté. Add corn and cook thoroughly. Sprinkle with grated cheese and heat until cheese melts. Do not stir. Serves 6.

❖─────────────────❖─────────────────❖

VERMICELLI ESPAÑOL
SPANISH VERMICELLI

Vermicelli may seem like an unusual ingredient for a Mexican recipe but it is simply delicious. Try it out on your family.

INGREDIENTS:

1 package vermicelli
2 cups chicken broth, or water
1 onion, diced

2 tomatoes, peeled and chopped
1/2 cup grated cheese
1 teaspoon salt and pepper

Lightly brown the vermicelli in the hot oil, breaking if necessary, and set aside. Combine onion, tomato, broth, salt and pepper in a medium pot. Bring to a boil and add vermicelli. Cover and simmer over low heat until all liquid has been cooked. Garnish with cheese. Serves 4.

❖─────────────────❖─────────────────❖

MACARON MEXICANA
MEXICAN MACARONI

INGREDIENTS:

8 ounces macaroni
2 ancho chiles, cleaned, peeled and seeded.
1 cup whipping cream

1/2 teaspoon salt
1 cup Monterey Jack cheese, shredded
Paprika

Preheat oven to 350°F. Cook macaroni until tender, following package directions. Drain. Place chiles in a blender and add cream and salt. Blend until chiles are finely chopped. In a greased casserole dish layer cooked macaroni, cheese, and sauce. Sprinkle with paprika. Bake for 30 minutes.

BOLAS DE PAPA
POTATO BALLS

Even though I prefer rice and beans to potatoes, the Irish in me comes out occasionally and I must have potatoes! These potato balls certainly do the trick.

INGREDIENTS:

3 medium baked potatoes
1/2 cup water
3 tablespoons butter
2 eggs

1/2 cup flour
Oil for frying
Salt
Pepper

While potatoes are hot, scrape out insides and mash smooth. Measure 2 cups of potatoes and place in a pan. Add boiling water, butter and flour all at once. Mix well until mixture separates from side of the pan. Add eggs, unbeaten, one at a time and beat well. Add salt and pepper to taste. Shape into balls and deep fry in hot oil until lightly brown. Makes 20 balls.

❖———————————————❖———————————————❖

CALABAZA ENMIELADA
SQUASH WITH BROWN SUGAR

Here's a way to get your children to love squash. Of course, with the brown sugar syrup this could almost be dessert!

INGREDIENTS:

1 4 to 6 pound banana squash
1 pound brown sugar

1/4 cup water
1/2 teaspoon vanilla

Clean the outside of the squash by rinsing with warm water and toweling dry. Cut squash into quarters and remove seeds. Tightly pack brown sugar on top of each piece of squash. Put in a pan and pour the combined water and vanilla over all. Cover tightly and cook over medium heat until the squash becomes tender. Place each section in a bowl and pour syrup over the top. Serves 2.

❖———————————————❖———————————————❖

NOPALES
CACTUS LEAVES

Nopales, the leaves of the nopal cactus, have a tart flavor similar to green pepper and can be found in most Mexican stores in cans or fresh.

HOW TO PREPARE NOPALES:

When preparing fresh nopales, carefully cut off all needles, using gloves and tongs. When needles have been removed, peel and dice and cook in hot oil with onion to flavor. Or, cook with hot chile sauce and onions and seasoning with salt and pepper to taste.

COLACHE
Mexican Succotash

My good friend Cathy is a vegetarian who loves Succotash, any way it is prepared. This is the Mexican variation of her own recipe.

INGREDIENTS:

3 medium zucchini, sliced
1 medium onion, chopped
1 green pepper, seeded and diced
1/4 cup canned pimiento, diced

2 large tomatoes, peeled, seeded and chopped
1 1/2 cups corn, fresh or frozen
1/4 cup butter
Salt and pepper

In a large skillet sauté onion in butter until tender. Add zucchini, onion, green pepper, pimiento, tomatoes and corn. If mixture is too dry, add either 1/2 cup water or chicken broth. Add salt and pepper to taste and simmer until vegetables are tender. Serves 6.

❖ ――――――――――― ❖ ――――――――――― ❖

AGUACATE CON TOMATILLO RELLENO
Avocado with Tomato Stuffing

On hot summer days, these stuffed avocados make a cool, yet elegant meal. Serve with a bowl of Gazpacho soup and a glass of Sangria.

INGREDIENTS:

2 large avocados
2 tablespoons lemon juice
2 tomatoes, peeled, seeded and diced
4 scallions, diced
1/2 teaspoon basil
4 green olives, chopped

4 tablespoons olive oil
1 1/2 tablespoons vinegar
1 teaspoon sugar
4 tablespoons mayonnaise
Cayenne pepper
1/2 head of lettuce
Salt and pepper

Peel the avocados and cut in half, lengthwise. Remove the pit and brush avocados with lemon juice to prevent browning. Combine oil, basil, vinegar, sugar, salt and pepper to taste and a pinch of cayenne pepper, mixing well. Add tomatoes, scallions, and olives to the oil mixture and add mayonnaise, blending well. Fill avocados with mixture and serve on a bed of lettuce. Garnish with a pinch of Cayenne pepper. Serves 4.

❖ ――――――――――― ❖ ――――――――――― ❖

A WORD ABOUT BAY LEAVES

Bay leaves come from evergreen trees in the Mediterranean area, or from the California laurel. Because they require a lot of simmering before their flavor permeates food, they should be added early on when used in cooking. The leaves hold their shape and texture and do not disintegrate during the cooking process and should always be removed before serving.

BEBIDAS
BEVERAGES

No Mexican fiesta is complete without a plentiful selection of delicious bebidas. Mexico has brought us such world renown drinks as Kahlua, Tequila and the always popular Margarita, a wonderful accompaniment to serve with those fiery Mexican dishes.

❖————————————————❖————————————————❖

MARGARITA

This is the quintessential Mexican drink. Served with tortilla chips and salsa while enjoying good friends and sunny weather you can experience the pleasures of Mexican entertaining.

INGREDIENTS:

4 ounces tequila
2 ounces Triple Sec

2 cups crushed ice
Lime wedges

Combine Tequila and Triple Sec and pour over crushed ice. Mix thoroughly. Using a wedge of lime, coat the rims of the Margarita glasses being used and dip in loose salt to coat edges. Pour the Margarita mixture into glasses and place a wedge of lime on each glass. Serves 4.

❖————————————————❖————————————————❖

TEPACHE
PINEAPPLE PUNCH

This exotic drink takes a little time to create, but the results are certainly worth the effort!

INGREDIENTS

1 large fresh pineapple
3 quarts water
2 cups barley

8 cups sugar
1 stick cinnamon
8 cloves

Chop and grind pineapple, including skin, and add water, cloves and cinnamon. Let mixture stand in a large pot for 2 days at room temperature. Boil barley in a quart of water until grains burst. Let cool before adding to pineapple mixture. Stir in sugar and ferment, in a dark place, for two days. Strain mixture and serve over ice. Makes 6 to 8 glasses.

From left: Margarita, Tequila Sunrise,
Tepache and Licuado de Fresa.

SORBETE ACAPULCO
SHERBET ACAPULCO

This is a very tasty drink that is great for warm days. Omit the alcohol when serving to children.

INGREDIENTS:

1 1/2 pints lemon sherbet
1/4 cup lime juice
4 tablespoons rum

5 tablespoons tequila
Peeled orange sections

Soften sherbet and add lime juice, rum and tequila. Mix well and refreeze. Scoop mixture into individual glasses and place a fresh orange section in each glass. Serves 4.

❖————————————❖————————————❖

SANGRIA
WINE COOLER

Not only is this a great drink to serve at any time, it adds a beautiful touch when served in a large punch bowl

INGREDIENTS:

1 bottle dry red wine
1 cup orange juice
1 7 ounce bottle club soda

1 lime, sliced
1 orange, sliced
2 cups fresh pineapple, cubed

Combine wine, lime slices, orange slices and pinapple cubes and chill. Add club soda before serving and pour over ice. Serves 6.

❖————————————❖————————————❖

LICUADO DE FRESA
STRAWBERRY DRINK

Using fresh strawberries is the secret to this zippy, frothy drink. If serving to children, omit the alcohol and blend with ice.

INGREDIENTS:

4 cups fresh strawberries
2 ounces tequila

1 cup water

Clean strawberries and remove stems. Place strawberries in a blender and purée, adding tequila and water. Chill for at least 1/2 hour. Pour over ice and serve. Place whole strawberry in glass for garnish. Serves 4.

LICUADO DE COCO
COCONUT DRINK

The flavor of coconuts make popular hot weather drinks and this frothy, flavorful drink is no exception.

INGREDIENTS:

2 cups coconut milk
2 cups gin
5 tablespoons sugar

1 7 ounce bottle club soda
Juice from 2 lemons
Ice

Mix together milk, gin, sugar, lemon juice and ice. Shake well and drain into tall glasses. Top with chilled club soda and stir. Serves 6.

TEQUILA DEL SOL
TEQUILA SUNRISE

There have been songs, movies and colors named after this drink. Tequila Sunrises have the same mellow ambiance as Mexico itself.

INGREDIENTS:

2 ounces tequila
1/2 cup orange juice
1 tablespoon grenadine

1 teaspoon lime juice
Maraschino Cherry
Ice

Mix tequila, orange and lime juices and grenadine in a blender. Pour into tall glasses and add ice. Garnish with Maraschino cherry.

CHOCOLAT MEXICANO
MEXICAN HOT CHOCOLATE

If Mexican chocolate is unavailable, use American sweet chocolate and add a dash of cinnamon.

INGREDIENTS:

4 cups milk
4 oz Mexican chocolate, grated
1/2 cup cream

2 tablespoons sugar
1/2 teaspoon cinnamon
1 egg yolk

Heat 1 cup milk and add chocolate. Stir until chocolate melts. Add remaining milk. Mix egg yolk with cream, add sugar and cinnamon. Combine with hot milk and simmer, stirring constantly. When hot, remove from heat and beat with mixer until a layer of foam coats the top. Serve hot.

POSTRES Y PANES
DESSERTS AND BREADS

People in the Mexican culture love celebrations. They celebrate many of the same special days as we North Americans do, such as Christmas, Independence Day (known as Cinco de Mayo), and birthdays, christenings and weddings. They have special foods for each of these events and an important part of any celebration, even the celebration of everyday life includes desserts. They are particularly fond of milk desserts and Flan is one of their favorites as well as one of the most famous. Enjoy these recipes and share them with the people who make your life worth celebrating.

❖———————————————❖———————————————❖

FLAN
CUSTARD

INGREDIENTS:

8 eggs
1 3/4 cups sugar

2 teaspoons vanilla
2 large cans evaporated milk

Melt 1 cup sugar in deep pan, stirring constantly until sugar turns golden. Coat the bottom of the pan with carmel and cool. Beat eggs, add vanilla remaining sugar, and milk, mixing well. Strain mixture into the pan with carmel and cover. Place pan into a larger pot containing hot water. Bake custard at 350°F for 45 minutes to 1 hour, or until a knife inserted in the center of the custard comes out clean. Chill for several hours and turn out on a platter. Serves 8.

❖———————————————❖———————————————❖

CAJETA DE CAMOTE CON PIÑA
SWEET POTATO PUDDING

INGREDIENTS:

2 cups sweet potato, cooked
and mashed
1 cup crushed pineapple
1 teaspoon cinnamon
1/2 teaspoon ground cloves

1/4 teaspoon salt
3/4 cup ground almonds
1 cup sugar
Whipped cream

Combine sweet potato, sugar, pineapple, cinnamon, cloves, almonds and salt, mix well. Cook over low heat, stirring often. When the mixture looses its shine and becomes a mass, move to a serving dish and garnish with whipped cream. Serve hot or cold. Serves 6

A selection of desserts and sweet breads.

ROSCA DE REYES
KINGS BREAD RING

The Kings Bread Ring is traditionally served on All Kings' Day, January 6. The person who gets the coin in his serving hosts a party on February 2.

INGREDIENTS:

4 1/2 cups all purpose flour
2 packages dry yeast
1 1/2 teaspoons orange peel, grated
1/4 cup butter, melted

1 cup warm milk
1/3 cup butter
1/3 cup sugar
3 eggs, beaten
2 teaspoons salt

INGREDIENTS FOR ICING:

1 to 2 tablespoons milk
1 1/3 cups powdered sugar
1 teaspoon rum flavoring

7 candied cherries, chopped
10 candied orange peel strips, 2 to 3 inches long

Dissolve yeast into milk by stirring. Cream sugar and 1/3 cup butter. Blend in salt and orange peel. Add yeast mixture, 1 egg and enough flour to make the dough stiff. Place dough on a lightly floured surface and knead until smooth and elastic, approximately 10 minutes. Put dough in greased bowl and grease top. Cover dough and it let rise until it doubles in size. Punch down. Knead until smooth, about 2 minutes. Roll dough into long strand and place on greased baking sheet. Shape into ring and seal ends together. Take a coin and push it into dough, making sure to cover it completely. Brush lightly with melted butter and cover. Let rise until it doubles, approximately 1 1/2 hours. Bake at 375°F for 30 minutes or until golden. While bread is cooling, combine powdered sugar, milk and rum flavoring. Beat until smooth and frost cooled bread. Decorate with candied fruit. Serves 12.

❖————————————————❖————————————————❖

PIÑA CON TEQUILA
TEQUILA PINEAPPLE

Tequila is my favorite import from Mexico and I like to serve this to my friends who think Tequila is only good for drinking.

INGREDIENTS:

8 slices of pineapple
1/2 cup sugar

4 ounces white Tequila
1 quart vanilla ice cream

Dredge pineapple slices through the sugar and place in a pan over heat. Cook pineapple until golden brown on both sides. Ignite the tequila and pour on the pineapple. Boil for three minutes. Serve over ice cream.

104

PASTELITOS DE BODA
MEXICAN WEDDING CAKES

This is another Mexican sweet that reflects the joy and happiness they feel for life. This is baked not only for weddings, but all year round.

INGREDIENTS:

1 cup butter
1/3 cup sugar
2 1/2 cups flour, sifted
1 teaspoon almond flavoring

1 cup pecans, copped fine
Red food coloring
Green food coloring
Salt

Blend butter and sugar in bowl until smooth. Add almond flavoring and stir. Add flour, nuts and dash of salt and mix well. Separate dough into halves and add three or four drops of green food coloring to one half and red to the other half. Chill all dough for 3 hours. Form small balls with dough and place on greased cookie sheet. Use a covered glass bottom to flatten each ball to 1/4 inch thickness. Preheat oven to 375°F and cook for 12 to 15 minutes, or until edge of cookies turn light brown. Makes 36.

❖─────────────────❖─────────────────❖

PASTEL DE PAN DE ELOTE
CORNBREAD PIE

INGREDIENTS:

1 cup margarine, softened
1 cup sugar
1 17 ounce can cream corn
1 cup Monterey Jack cheese, shredded
4 eggs

1 4 ounce can green chiles, drained, seeded, and chopped
1 cup yellow cornmeal
1 cup flour,
4 teaspoons baking powder
1/2 teaspoon salt

Cream butter and sugar until light and fluffy. Beat in eggs, one at a time. Stir in corn, cheese, chiles and cornmeal. Sift flour, baking powder and salt and stir into batter. Preheat oven to 300°F. Pour mixture into greased 13x9 inch baking pan and bake for 1 hour, until a wooden pick inserted in center comes out clean. Serve hot. Serves 8.

❖─────────────────❖─────────────────❖

A WORD ABOUT DESSERTS:

Mexicans are known for having a sweet tooth and Mexican cooks always serve their family and guests some sort of after meal sweet. Sometimes this will consist of a simple bowl of fruit with sweet cream. Often something a little more elaborate, such as the ever popular flan or a delectable bread pudding is served.

PASTEL DE ARROZ
RICE CAKE

Serve this delicious and easy to make Rice Cake with a fresh fruit topping such as strawberries or fresh peaches.

INGREDIENTS:

1 1/2 cups regular rice flour	2 teaspoons baking powder
1/2 pound butter, softened	1/2 cup Monterey Jack cheese,
1 1/4 cups sugar	shredded
5 medium eggs	1/2 cup milk

Grease and flour a 9 inch square baking pan, set aside. Preheat oven to 350°F. Beat butter until soft. Add sugar and beat until fluffy. Add one egg at a time, beating after each addition. Sift rice flour and baking powder into butter mixture. Stir in cheese and milk. Turn mixture into prepared pan. Bake for 35 to 40 minutes, until cake bounces back when touched with finger. Cool cake in pan on a rack for 15 minutes. Take cake from pan and let sit on rack until cool. Top with fresh fruit. Serves 6.

❖————————————❖————————————❖

BUÑUELOS
FRITTERS

Fritters are often eaten at the early morning breakfast, *desayuno,* along with coffee or a glass of milk.

INGREDIENTS:

1/2 cup sugar	2 eggs
1/4 teaspoon salt	3 tablespoons rum
1 cup water	Oil for frying
4 3/4 cups flour, sifted	

INGREDIENTS FOR COATING:

1 teaspoon cinnamon	1/2 cup sugar

Mix flour, 1/2 cup sugar and salt in large bowl. Beat eggs, water and rum together and add to flour mixture. Mix to form a stiff dough. Place dough on floured board and knead for 2 minutes until smooth. Cut dough into 4 sections. Roll sections on floured pastry cloth until there are 4 rectangles 10x15 inches. Cut into 2x5 inch strips. Twist two strips of dough together to form fritters. Heat oil to 370° F in a skillet. Mix 1/2 cup sugar and cinnamon together in a shallow pan and set aside. Fry dough until golden and place on paper towel to drain excess liquid. Dip in cinnamon sugar and coat. Makes 40.

TAMALES DULCES
DESSERT TAMALES

The date-nut filling makes these tamales a temptingly tasty treat. Make them when you make regular tamales and serve as dessert.

INGREDIENTS:

3 1/2 dozen dry corn husks	1 cup brown sugar
4 cups masa harina flour,	1/2 teaspoon cinnamon
1 cup lard	1/4 cup butter
1 cup sugar	1 cup pitted dates, chopped
1 teaspoon salt	1 cup pecans, chopped

In a large saucepan cover corn husks with boiling water. Soak for at least 30 minutes. Beat lard until fluffy, using mixer. Combine masa flour, sugar and salt. Gradually add the flour and sugar mixture to lard and add water until dough sticks together and has a pastelike consistency. To prepare date filling; blend brown sugar, butter and cinnamon until smooth. Dry husks by placing on paper towels and patting. Add chopped dates and pecans and mix evenly. Spread 2 tablespoons tamale dough on center portion of husk, leaving at least a 2 inch margin at both ends and about a 1/2 inch margin at the right side. Spoon 1 1/2 tablespoons filling onto dough. Wrap tamale, overlapping left side first, then right side slightly over left. Fold bottom up and top down. Lay tamales in top section of steamer with open flaps on bottom. Tie with string if husks are too short to stay closed. Tamales may completely fill the top section of steamer but should be placed so there are spaces between them for the circulation of steam. Steam over simmering water for 1 hour, until corn husks can be peeled from dough easily. Makes 3 1/2 dozen tamales.

❖————————————————❖————————————————❖

PLATANOS BORRACHOS
BANANAS WITH RUM

An easy, yet elegant, dessert to make when entertaining guests. Serve with freshly brewed coffee.

INGREDIENTS:

6 ripe bananas,	1/2 stick butter
1 teaspoon vanilla extract	1/2 cup brown sugar
1 cup almonds, chopped	2 tablespoons rum
1 cup raisins	1 cup whipped cream

Mix vanilla, almonds and raisins. Set aside. Cook butter and sugar over medium heat until melted. Add sliced bananas and cook until tender. Remove from heat and add rum, stirring gently. Top with whipped cream

CAPIROTADA
MEXICAN BREAD PUDDING

It seems that almost every culture has its own version of bread pudding. This is the Mexican version, and a very good one at that!

INGREDIENTS:

1 pound brown sugar	1 clove
1 cup raisins	1/2 cup peanuts, chopped
1 cinnamon stick	1 cup almonds, blanched and
1 quart water	chopped
6 pieces of toast, cubed	1/2 pound Monterey Jack
3 medium apples, sliced	cheese, cubed

Mix water, sugar, clove and cinnamon stick together and bring to a boil. Grease a casserole dish and place a layer of bread cubes on the bottom. Layer with apple slices and sprinkle part of the nuts, raisins and cheese. Keep layering until all ingredients are gone. Remove cinnamon and clove from syrup and pour over pudding. Bake at 350°F for 30 minutes. Serve hot. Can be garnished with a dollop of whipped cream. Serves 6.

❖――――――――――――❖――――――――――――❖

GALLETAS DE MOCA Y CEREZA
MOCHA CHERRY COOKIES

INGREDIENTS:

2 cups flour	1 cup butter, melted to room
1/2 cup sugar	temperature
2 teaspoons vanilla	1/2 cup maraschino cherries,
1/4 cup unsweetened cocoa	diced
1 tablespoon instant coffee	1/2 teaspoon salt
1 cup walnuts, chopped	1 box powdered sugar

Preheat oven to 325°F. Blend butter, sugar and vanilla until fluffy. Sift together cocoa, flour, instant coffee and salt. Add dry ingredients to butter mixture in small amounts until combined. Add nuts and cherries and chill. Using a teaspoon, shape dough into balls and place on a greased cookie sheet. Bake for 20 minutes. Sprinkle cookies with powdered sugar while warm. These are easily frozen. Makes 6 dozen.

❖――――――――――――❖――――――――――――❖

SOPAIPILLAS
MEXICAN DOUGHNUTS

Sopaipillas are often sold at carnivals and fairs all over the Southwest as well as by street vendors in Mexico.

INGREDIENTS:

2 cups flour
2 teaspoons baking powder
1 tablespoon shortening
1/2 teaspoon salt

3/4 cup warm water
Oil for frying
Honey

Mix flour, salt and baking powder in medium mixing bowl. Cut in shortening until evenly blended. Add warm water until all ingredients are moist. Place dough on a lightly floured surface. Knead for about 5 minutes until smooth. Wrap dough in plastic wrap and let sit for 30 minutes. Separate dough in half and roll each ball on a lightly floured board. Roll each ball into a circle about 1/8 inches thick. Cut into 8 pie-shaped pieces. Heat 1 1/2 inches of oil in a skillet to 400°F. Gently place wedges of dough in hot oil. Cook until puffy and golden brown, turning once. If wedges do not puff up right away, the oil is not hot enough. Place cooked sopaipillas on paper towel to drain excess oil. Serve warm with honey. Makes 16.

❖ ──────────── ❖ ──────── ❖

PAN DE ELOTE Y CHILES
BLUE CORN BREAD WITH CHILES

I just love cornbread and this recipe is special. As well as tasting lovely, its appearance on the plate is quite attractive.

INGREDIENTS:

1 1/2 cups blue cornmeal
1/2 cup flour
1/2 teaspoon salt
1 tablespoon baking powder
1/4 cup onion, chopped fine

1/2 cup butter, melted
3 jalapeño peppers, chopped
1 1/2 cups Monterey Jack cheese, shredded
1 cup milk

Preheat oven to 350°F. Combine flour, cornmeal, baking powder, onions and salt. Add milk and butter and mix thoroughly. In a separate bowl, combine cheese and jalapeños. Grease a medium sized baking pan and pour 1/2 of the batter into pan. Spread the cheese and jalapeño mixture evenly over batter. Pour remaining batter over cheese and cook for 1 hour. Let cool and cut into squares. Serves 8.

❖ ──────────── ❖ ──────── ❖

A WORD ABOUT CORN:

Corn is the oldest and most revered crop in the Mexican culture. The history of Mexico reflects the ancient Indians belief that man was created from corn by the gods. Today, corn is still considered one of the most important crops in Mexico and is used in everything from beverages to desserts. Masa is the corn dough used in the preparation of corn tortillas, considered to be the bread of Mexico.

BURRITOS DE MANZANA
APPLE BURRITO'S

This dessert is simply divine. The apple cinnamon filling is tasty enough to make this a prize winning selection.

INGREDIENTS:

8 Granny Smith apples, sliced
1 cup water
1 cup sugar
1/2 teaspoon cinnamon

1/8 teaspoon nutmeg
12 large flour tortillas
1 cup Cheddar cheese, shredded

Preheat oven to 350°F. Combine water, sugar, cinnamon and nutmeg and bring to a boil. Add apples and simmer on medium low heat until tender, but still firm. Drain apples, reserving juice. Divide the apple mixture and cheese equally on all tortillas. Spoon 3 teaspoons of syrup over apples and cheese and fold. In a buttered baking dish place filled tortillas, seam side down, and spoon remaining syrup over the top. Bake for 5 to 10 minutes. When tortillas begin to crisp, remove from oven. Serves 12.

❖────────────────❖────────────────❖

PAN DE ELOTE MEXICANO
MEXICAN CORNBREAD

Mild green chiles give this colorful cornbread its unique flavor. Serve with chile butter for an extra zing.

INGREDIENTS:

1 1/2 cups cornmeal
2 tablespoons bacon drippings
1 1/2 tablespoons flour
1 tablespoon salt
1/2 teaspoon baking soda
1 cup buttermilk
2/3 cup oil

2 eggs, beaten
1 8 ounce can cream corn
1 4 ounce can green chiles, drained and chopped
4 green onions, chopped
1 1/2 cups shredded Monterey Jack cheese

Mix cornmeal, flour, salt and baking soda in a mixing bowl. Add buttermilk, oil, eggs and corn and mix well. Stir in chiles and onions. Preheat oven to 375°F. Grease a large baking dish with bacon fat, heat in oven. Pour half the batter into heated pan and sprinkle with half the cheese. Repeat process using remaining batter and cheese. Bake for 35 minutes. Cut and serve warm. Serves 8.

❖────────────────❖────────────────❖

A WORD ABOUT MEXICAN CREAM:

Crema Natural is a slightly sour cream that thickens with age. *Crema Dulce* is a sweet cream very similar to our whipping cream.

BUDIN BORRACHO
DRUNKEN PUDDING

The brandy in this recipe gives it the "Drunken Pudding". You will be drunk with be pleasure when you taste this dish.

INGREDIENTS:

10 ladyfingers cookies	2 cups hot milk
1/2 cup brandy	1 teaspoon vanilla
6 egg yolks	1 cup whipped cream
1/4 cup sugar	1 cup almonds, chopped
1/4 teaspoon salt	Maraschino Cherries

In a medium bowl, break up ladyfingers. Sprinkle with liquor, set aside. Beat egg yolks with sugar and salt in the top of a double boiler. Gradually add hot milk to egg mixture. Cook over simmering water, stirring often, until mixture coats the back of a spoon. Remove from stove. Add vanilla and cool. Fold whipped cream and custard into ladyfinger mixture. Add nuts and chill. Garnish with cherries. Serves 8.

❖―――――――――――❖―――――――――――❖

EMPANADAS DE FRUTA
FRUIT EMPANADAS

Empanadas are a traditional Mexican dessert. Filled with fruit, these empanadas are a very popular sweet.

INGREDIENTS:

10 1/4 inch thick, 5 inch diameter uncooked flour tortillas (recipe page 40)	10 oz fresh papaya, cut in strips 2 8 ounce packages cream cheese, cut in 1/4x1 inch strips

Divide papaya and cream cheese strips evenly among tortillas. Fold the tortillas in half, allowing rounded edge of bottom half to extend about 1/4 inch beyond top half. Fold bottom edge up and over top about 1/2 inch. Crimp edges decoratively to seal. Pour 2 to 3 inches of oil into medium saucepan or deep fat fryer and heat to 375°F. Add empanadas one at a time and fry for 1 or 2 minutes or until golden brown on both sides. Spoon oil over top while cooking to encourage puffing. Using a slotted spoon, remove from pan and drain on paper towels. Dust with powdered sugar and serve. Makes 10.

❖―――――――――――❖―――――――――――❖

A WORD ABOUT EMPANADAS:
Empanadas are often filled with beef, chicken, pork and fish fillings.

INDEX